PRAYING IN THE PRESENCE OF

OUR LORD

FOR THE
HOLY
SOULS

PRAYING IN THE PRESENCE OF

OUR LORD

FOR THE
HOLY
SOULS

SUSAN TASSONE

FR. BENEDICT J. GROESCHEL, C.F.R.
SERIES EDITOR

Our Sunday Visitor Publishing Division
Our Sunday Visitor, Inc.
Huntington, Indiana 46750

Nihil Obstat
Rev. Charles R. Meyer, S.T.D.
Censor Deputatus

Imprimatur
The Most Rev. Raymond Goedert
Vicar General, Archdiocese of Chicago
August 15, 2001

The *nihil obstat* and *imprimatur* are official declarations of ecclesiastical
authority that a book is free of doctrinal or moral error. No
implication is contained therein that those who have granted the *nihil
obstat* or *imprimatur* agree with the content, opinions, or statements
expressed in the work. Nor do they assume any legal responsibility
associated with publication.

With an exception or two, the Scripture citations used in this work are
taken from the *Holy Bible, Revised Standard Version, Catholic Edition*,
copyright © 1965 and 1966 by the Division of Christian Education of the
National Council of the Churches of Christ in the U.S.A., and are used
by permission of the copyright holder; all rights reserved. The author and
publisher are grateful to those publishers and others whose materials,
whether in the public domain or protected by copyright laws, have been
used in one form or another in this volume. Some text has been slightly
modified for the sake of clarity and other considerations. Every reasonable
effort has been made to determine copyright holders of excerpted
materials and to secure permissions as necessary. If any copyrighted
materials have been inadvertently used in this work without proper credit
being given in one form or another, please notify Our Sunday Visitor in
writing so that future printings of this work may be corrected accordingly.

ISBN: 978-0-87973-921-8
LCCCN: 2001-135239

Cover design by Tyler Ottinger
Cover photo of The Poor Souls Shrine at St. Michael's Church
(Old Town), Chicago, by George E. Robertson
Back-cover photo courtesy
Servizio Fotografico de L'Osservatore Romano
PRINTED IN THE UNITED STATES OF AMERICA

To my friend and greatest blessing,
Steven Jay Gross,
who, like the holy souls,
constantly urges me on
to heavenly heights!

Acknowledgments

There is a saying that goes: "If you ever see a turtle on a fence post, you know it did not get there by itself."

Special thanks to the research staff at: University of St. Mary of the Lake, Mundelein, Illinois; Loyola University Chicago, Chicago, Illinois; Catholic Theological Union, Chicago, Illinois; and Dominican University, River Forest, Illinois.

Their help was invaluable in locating rare text.

I am particularly grateful to the following for the use of their material:

Assist the Souls in Purgatory, copyright © 1955 by the Benedictine Convent of Perpetual Adoration, Clyde, Missouri.

Early Christian Prayers, edited by A. Hamman, O.F.M., and translated by Walter Mitchell, published by Henry Regnery Co., Chicago, Illinois, English translation copyright © 1961 by Longmans, Green and Co. Ltd., London, England.

Eucharistic Reflections, by Rt. Rev. Msgr. William Reyna, adapted by Winfrid Herbst, S.D.S. (from the German translation by Ottilie Boediker), copyright © 1957 by The Newman Press, Westminster, Maryland.

Holy Hour, by The Rev. Mateo Crawley-Boevey, SS. CC., copyright © 1944 by the National Center of the Enthronement, Fathers of the Sacred Hearts, Fairhaven, Massachusetts.

Lest We Forget, by Very Rev. James Alberione, S.S.P., S.T.D., copyright © 1967 by the Daughters of St. Paul, Boston, Massachusetts.

The Mystery of Purgatory, by Father Hubert, O.F.M.,

I hope this book gives the faithful a means to reach out to their loved ones and speed their journey home to heaven. And so I say, "All the glory to God, forever!"

GUSTAVE DORÉ'S "RESURRECTION OF LAZARUS"

Table of Contents

Foreword
by Francis Cardinal George, O.M.I. / 9

Introduction
by Father Benedict J. Groeschel, C.F.R. / 10

Preface: How to Pray for the Dead / 17

Prayers for the Faithful Departed / 19

Psalms / 39

Supplications to Mary, Queen of Heaven / 55

Holy Hour Prayers / 77

Invoking the Saintly Ones / 109

Prayers for Specific People / 125

Novena Prayers for Every Day / 163

About the Author / 176

Foreword

The risen Lord is free of all constraints imposed by space and time. He can be anywhere he wants to be, and he wants to be entirely present to us in the Blessed Sacrament of the Altar. Under the appearance of bread, Jesus is truly present: divinity and humanity, body and soul. When the faithful spend time with him in adoration, their love for the Lord grows strong.

Love for Jesus inspires love for all those whom Jesus himself loves, whether living or dead. Bringing all those we love before the Lord in the Blessed Sacrament, he will move us to pray for the souls in purgatory. He loves them, and he wants us to pray for them. These prayers, collected by Susan Tassone, show us how to pray for them. I recommend this book; most of all, I recommend prayer before the Blessed Sacrament for the souls in purgatory.

Francis Cardinal George, O.M.I.
Archbishop of Chicago

Introduction

One of the most cherished devotions of Catholics has been fervent prayer for their deceased family, friends, and that vast multitude of people who have left this world on their way to Our Father's House. In fact, all Christians, except some Protestants, and almost all people of other world religions — including Jews, Muslims, Buddhists, and Hindus — prayerfully remember their dead in one way or another. Archeological examination of ancient tombs indicates that in the first centuries of Christianity the followers of Christ and His apostles invoked the name of God and His Son's on those who were making their way from this world to heaven. There was no sense in praying for them if they were already there. This means that they were praying for them on their journey to the kingdom of heaven after death. Long before St. Augustine asked the readers of his *Confessions* to pray for his deceased parents, Christians made devout intercession to the martyrs, asking them to pray for them in the kingdom of God. At the same time Christians prayed *for* the rest of the deceased. They did not pray to those who were not martyrs and saints. St. Monica, the mother of Augustine, admonished her children to remember her prayerfully at the altar of God (*Confessions*, Book IX, 11).

Although Catholic and Eastern Orthodox Christians have somewhat different ideas about the journey of the soul to God, they both see it as an experience of expiation and purification, during which the soul, through God's grace and mercy and the precious blood of Jesus Christ, is prepared to enter into the fullness of God's eternal glory. Even Protestants like Samuel Johnson, author of the first complete English dictionary, could respond to those objecting to Catholic teaching on purgatory by saying that many of the dead are not ready to go into God's kingdom. We hope that these people are not going to hell, Dr. Johnson and others have reasoned, so "the Catholics must be right."

A number of quotations from the Bible were used by the early Fathers of the Church to describe the journey from death to life. Because of St. Paul's words in 1 Corinthians 3:12-15, there was an affirmation that there would be some purifying fire, although the Church Fathers knew that physical fire had no relevance to the purely spiritual being of souls without bodies. Catholic and Orthodox Christians have long used a quotation from 2 Maccabees 12:45: "It was a holy and pious thought," referring to the custom of offering prayers for the dead. An examination of the prayers in this book will dispel the illusion, often held by the uninformed, that our prayers or good works accomplish something directly for the holy souls, that somehow we can "buy their way out" of purgatory. Every prayer in this book explicitly, or at least implicitly, calls on God the Father in His mercy or on His Son, the Redeemer, to receive the holy souls and bring them into the kingdom.

Because of the consolation of faith in the immortality of the soul there is a very healthy and normal impulse to want to do something for our beloved dead. As Terence Cardinal Cooke used to say, "Prayer is the best gift we can give someone."

The gift of prayer for a dear one on the journey to eternal life is more important than a monument or flowers or any other kind of tribute. The Church has long believed that the very best we can do is to remember the holy souls very specially in the celebration of the Eucharistic Sacrifice of the Mass. In the Mass the one who prays is Christ the Eternal High Priest, and we join ourselves to Him. Just as it is really Christ who baptizes and absolves from sin and ministers to us in all of the sacraments, so it is clearly Christ who prays in His own words spoken by the priest, "This is my Body. . . . This is the cup of my Blood." What prayer can be more powerful than the prayer of Christ?

Along with remembering the dead in the Holy Sacrifice, it is beautiful and powerful to pray for our dear dead in the presence of Christ. We are reminded of Martha and Mary accompanying Jesus to the tomb of their brother Lazarus. The words of Martha, "I know that he will rise again in the resurrection at the last day" (John 11:24), echo in our souls as we pray and grieve for our beloved dead. I think that praying for the dead is one of the healthiest things we can do when we feel that death has robbed us of their presence. We can even speak to them if we wish, asking God to let them know what we say and that we remember them. And in what better place could we pray for the dead than before the Eucharist, where we can experience Our Blessed Savior present? If we pray in the presence of the Lord, are we not like Martha and Mary? Are we not also like the Magdalene, who was grieving at the tomb when she first met the risen Christ?

Susan Tassone has gone through the library of the Church's prayers and has selected a treasury of petitions for the dead. Some prayers are not even specifically for the dead but remind us of the great destiny of eternal life, like the *Te Deum* (a great hymn of praise to the Holy Trinity traditionally attributed to St. Ambrose or St. Nicetas of Remesiana), which begins this collection. Others are beautiful and solemn prayers of the Liturgy for the Dead. At times, Susan even uses the ideas of the journey to God coming from private revelations, like the writings of St. Gertrude.

In using the term "private revelations," it is important to note that we are in no way equating them with Sacred Scripture. The popes have consistently taught that such revelations are not infallible. The eighteenth-century Pope Benedict XIV cites private revelations, some written even by canonized saints, that contain serious errors. Those interested in reading more on this subject are referred to my little book *A Still, Small Voice* (Ignatius Press, 1992) for the Church's teaching on this subject. Pope Benedict stresses that private revelations are of no greater value than the writings of any other devout writer. Their statements are only as good as their arguments. In their powerful prayer and dialogue with the Lord, very holy souls often get some of their own ideas mixed up with the experience of the graces they are receiving.

The same thing is true of popular preachers. On the one hand, St. Alphonsus Liguori stressed the terrible pains of purgatory, while on the other hand, St. Catherine of Genoa, the great fifteenth-century mystic, wrote: "There is no joy other than that in paradise to be compared to the joy of the souls in purgatory." The reason for this is that the holy souls are in perfect charity. She continues: "The joy increases day by day because of the way in which the love of God corresponds to that of the soul, since the impediment to that love is worn away daily and this impediment is the rust of sin. As it is consumed, the soul is more and more open to God's love."

St. Catherine of Genoa is often misquoted. She does say that the souls in purgatory feel a fire like that of hell except that they have no sense of guilt. The similarity in the suffering is that in one case it holds the soul back temporarily from the vision of God. The lost souls feel "infinite blame and suffering."

St. Catherine is an important person on the topic of the souls in purgatory, and you might be interested to read her revelations. They have been published in *Catherine of Genoa: Purgation and Purgatory, The Spiritual Dialogue*, edited by Serge Hughes and me (Paulist Press, 1979).

Everyone agrees that purgatory is a time of preparation and that its greatest pain is the sorrow of not being united with the Holy Trinity in the eternal destiny we are called to. A devout Christian feels this pain even in this life as St. Paul says, "For I am already on the point of being sacrificed; the time of my departure has come. I have fought the good fight, I have finished the race, I have kept the faith. Henceforth there is laid up for me the crown of righteousness" (2 Timothy 4:6-8).

St. Catherine also reminds us that we have begun our purgatory even now. Personally, I don't want to arrive in purgatory before my time. But I certainly don't want to be late either.

How to Pray for the Holy Souls

It is obvious that Christian prayer from time immemorial has been explicit about praying for particular people. I pray, of course, for all the dear souls being led through the last stages of the journey to God; but my most fervent, heartfelt, and wholesome prayers are for those I miss, for those whose lives are changed and not ended — those whom I love and long to see again. I even pray for those who died long ago because we do not know how time in this world measures up with duration in the next. To paraphrase the Psalmist: "A thousand years shall be as a day."

I hope that soon I will join that great and penitential procession. Like St. Claude de la Colombière, the spiritual director of St. Margaret Mary, I want to be there for exactly as long as God wants me. "Into your hands, O Lord, I commend my spirit." I know from my daily sinfulness that I am certainly not ready to enter into the pure radiance of eternity. Surely Our Savior has accomplished all we need for salvation, but I have not yet opened my heart to all that He wants me to be as His disciple. That enemy — myself — is still very much in the way. So as I trust Him in this life, I will trust Him in the next.

Any good Christian should be busy trying to give comfort to the suffering. How about your own family and friends who have gone before you? Follow St. Monica's advice: Pray for them at the altar of God.

And don't be sad about it all. The Ven. John Henry Newman wrote a marvelous poem, *The Dream of Gerontius* (Alba House, 2001), in which he applies St. Catherine's teaching to the experience of an old man from the moment of death until his entrance into purgatory. His guardian angel accompanies him, and as he enters into the purifying bath of purgatory, the angel says to him: "Farewell, but not forever! brother dear, / Be brave and patient on thy bed of sorrow; / Swiftly shall pass thy night of trial here, / And I will come and wake thee on the morrow."

FATHER BENEDICT J. GROESCHEL, C.F.R.

"If I forget those who are no more, / I shall be forgotten in my turn" (Prince Napoleon, Camden Court).

Preface: How to Pray for the Dead

St. Gertrude: Make known to me, most loving Lord, by what labors or prayers Thy mercy could be moved to grant that those souls should be freed from the hideous burden which debars from the suffrages of the Church.

To whom the Lord replied: In the course of time the intolerable load may be alleviated by certain prayers and labors undertaken with a faithful intention by their friends; and that sooner or later according to the more or less earnest devotion of the faithful living who make the offer; and also according to the merit which the intercessors have acquired. Certainly I am as much gratified as though I Myself were the liberated captive every time that through your intercession one of those souls is released.

Lord, in union with the love with which Thou, the Creator of all things, didst deign for the salvation of men to be judged; in union with the confidence with which, having destroyed the empire of death and rising victorious from the dead and ascending into heaven, Thou hast exalted human nature to the right hand of God; and in union with the joy with which all the saints rejoice that through Thy Incarnation, Passion, and Resurrection they are among the blessed; I offer to Thee these acts of devotion.

Prayers for the
Faithful Departed

Te Deum

(This song of praise is still used
in the Divine Office.)

You are God: we praise you;
You are the Lord: we acclaim you;
You are the eternal Father:
All creation worships you.
To you all angels, all the powers of heaven,
Cherubim and Seraphim, sing in endless
    praise:
Holy, holy, holy, Lord, God of power and
    might,
heaven and earth are full of your glory.
The glorious company of apostles praise
    you.
The noble fellowship of prophets praise
    you.
The white-robed army of martyrs praise
    you.
Throughout the world the holy Church
    acclaims you:
Father, of majesty unbounded,
your true and only Son, worthy of all
    worship,
and the Holy Spirit, advocate and guide.
You, Christ, are the king of glory,
the eternal Son of the Father.
When you became man to set us free
you did not spurn the Virgin's womb.

You overcame the sting of death,
and opened the kingdom of heaven to all
believers.
You are seated at God's right hand in glory.
We believe that you will come, and be our
judge.
Come then, Lord, and help your people,
bought with the price of your own blood,
and bring us with your saints to glory
everlasting.

"Awake, O sleeper, and arise from the dead, and Christ shall give you light" (Ephesians 5:14).

Early Christians "asked that the departed, or the 'sleepers,' as they called them, may receive forgiveness, life, rest and peace, and that they may be one with God, or with Christ."

To the faithful, "the dead are more alive than the living; . . . they ask for intercession of the dead and beg them to remember their brethren who are still waiting for God to call them to him. Parents are found invoking their children."

A Dead Man's Prayer to the Living

Holy, holy, holy. Hail to you who still have the consolation of seeing the light of Our Father who is in heaven. Pray that we may have rest in Christ Jesus, Our Lord, and in his life-giving Spirit. May you receive the grace to spend your lives well before you leave this world; for even I, poor thing that I am, having lived the short space of life allotted to me, possess my share of what God has promised us.

The Intercession of the Dead

Pray for your parents.
Pray for your children.
May he pray for us.
Pray for us. Pray that we may be saved.
Pray for the one child you have left behind.
Live in Christ and pray for us.

O Lord Jesus Christ, King of Glory
(This prayer is from the Roman Missal.)

O Lord Jesus Christ, King of glory, deliver the souls of all the faithful departed from the pains of hell and from the bottomless pit; deliver them out of the lion's mouth, lest hell should swallow them up, lest they fall into the outer darkness; but let Thy standard-bearer, St. Michael, bring them back into Thy holy light, which Thou didst promise of old to Abraham and to his seed. Amen.

Blest Are the Pure in Heart
(This is from Pope John Paul II, at the Verano Cemetery, Rome, November 1, 1981.)

For all our brothers and sisters who rest in the Verano Cemetery and in all the graveyards of Rome and of the world, may the words of Christ in the Sermon on the Mount become the Good News of eternal salvation.

May the kingdom of heaven be theirs.
May they possess it as a "Promised Land."
May they have eternal joy.
May they be satisfied in their hunger and
thirst for righteousness.
May they be called children of God forever.
May they see God face to face.
May their joy and happiness be full and
unlimited.
Let us pray:

O God, the glory of believers and the life of the just who saved us by the death and resurrection of your Son, be merciful to our deceased brothers and sisters. When they were in our midst they professed faith in the resurrection; give them endless bliss. Through Christ our Lord. Amen.

Solace for the Souls

Have mercy, O gentle Jesus, on the souls detained in purgatory. You who for their ransom did take upon yourself our human nature and suffer the most cruel death, pity their sighs and the tears shed when they raise their longing eyes toward you. And by virtue of your Passion, cancel the penalty due to their sins. May your Blood, O tender Jesus, your precious Blood, descend into purgatory to solace and refresh those who there languish in captivity. Reach forth your hand to them, and lead them into the realms of refreshment, light, and peace. Amen.

Prayer of St. Gertrude the Great
(Dictated by Our Lord to St. Gertrude
to release numerous souls from
purgatory each time it is said.)

Eternal Father, I offer Thee the most precious Blood of Thy Divine Son, Jesus, in union with all the Masses said throughout the world today, for all the holy souls in purgatory, for sinners everywhere, for sinners in the Universal Church, those in my own home and within my family. Amen.

Act of Love
(The seraphic ardors of this Franciscan prayer
propose it as an act of love well suited
to help the holy souls.)

I beseech Thee, O Lord, that the fiery and sweet strength of Thy love may absorb my soul from all things that are under heaven, that I may die for love of Thy love as Thou didst die for love of my love.

Godly Abode
(From the Coptic Liturgy of St. Gregory.)

Remember, O Lord, all those who fell asleep and rested while in the priesthood, and those who were in any order of the laity. Grant a resting place to their souls in the bosom of our fathers Abraham, Isaac, and Jacob; feed them in a green pasture, by the waters of comfort, in the paradise of joy, the place from which the broken heart, sorrow, and sighs flee away, in the light of Thy saints.

Yea, Lord, make them rest in that abode; and us also, who are sojourners in this place. Keep us in Thy faith, and grant us Thy peace unto the end.

O happy Virgin, thro' thee was heaven won,
By thy sufferings with the Lamb Who made us
*   all,*
By thy vigil at the tomb of thy Beloved Son,
Through this Office ransom all our souls.

Office of the Dead
(From the first letter of the Apostle Paul
to the Corinthians 15:51-57.)

Now I am going to tell you a mystery. Not all of us shall fall asleep, but all of us are to be changed — in an instant, the twinkling of an eye, at the sound of the last trumpet. The trumpet will sound and the dead will be raised incorruptible, and we shall be changed. This corruptible body must be clothed with incorruptibility, this mortal body with immortality. When the corruptible frame takes on incorruptibility and the mortal immortality, then will the saying of Scripture be fulfilled: "Death is swallowed up in victory." "O death, where is your victory? O death, where is your sting?" The sting of death is sin, and sin gets its power from the law. But thanks be to God who has given us the victory through our Lord Jesus Christ.

Prayer for the Most Abandoned Souls

Have mercy, we beseech you, Lord God, through the precious Passion of your only begotten Son, our Lord, Jesus Christ; have mercy on those souls that have no intercessor to you to have them in remembrance, which have neither hope nor comfort in their torments, but only for that they be framed after your image and likeness and ensigned with the sign of faith, which either by negligence of them that be living or by long process of time are forgotten by their friends and posterity.

Spare them, Lord, and defend your creation; neither despise the work of your hands, but extend your right hand to them and deliver them from duress of their pains and bring them into the company of the celestial citizens through your exceeding great mercies which are most excellent above all your works.

Who lives and reigns in unity with the Holy Spirit, one God forever and ever. Amen.

Have pity on me, you at least my friends!
No, not with death, true love, true pity ends.
Your prayers can still assist me on my way.
Take pity on me, O dear friends and pray,
For the Hand of the Lord has touched me!

Perfect Peace
(From the Coptic Liturgy.)

To these, O Lord, and to all those of whom we make remembrance, and to those also of whom each one thinks in his own heart, give rest in the bosom of Abraham, Isaac, and Jacob. Give them refreshment in the smiling fields of the Paradise of peace where there is neither sorrow nor pain. Grant to them the good things Thou hast promised, which eye has not seen nor ear heard. They have indeed sinned through ignorance and forgetfulness, for they were but men, living in this world and weighed down by the burden of a fleshly nature. O Thou who art a God of goodness and the friend of man, deign to pardon them, for there is no man on earth, even if his life were but of one day, who is not stained with sin.

"Imagine all the torments in the world, you will not find one equal to the privation of the Beatific Vision" (St. John Chrysostom).

Prayer of Cleansing

O Lord, who art ever merciful and bounteous with Thy gifts, look down upon the suffering souls in purgatory. Remember not their offenses and negligences, but be mindful of Thy loving mercy, which is from all eternity.

Cleanse them of their sins and fulfill their ardent desires that they may be made worthy to behold Thee face to face in Thy glory. May they soon be united with Thee and hear those blessed words which call them to their heavenly home, "Come, blessed of My Father, take possession of the Kingdom prepared for you from the foundation of the world."

Ascend to God!
(By St. Gertrude.)

Hail, all ye faithful souls of Jesus Christ! May He give you rest who is the One True Rest. May Jesus Christ, who for us men and for our salvation was born of a pure Virgin, and redeemed you with

His precious Blood, bless you, and release you from your discipline of watching and expectation, and raise you up in the Day of Judgment and place you with His saints and angels.

> *"I do not believe it would be possible to find any joy comparable to that of a soul in purgatory, except the joy of the blessed in Paradise — a joy which goes on increasing day by day as God more and more flows in upon the soul, which He does abundantly in proportion at every hindrance is consumed away. . . . Indeed as far as the will is concerned, the pains are not pains at all, so contentedly do the souls rest in the ordinance of God to whose will pure love unites them"* (St. Catherine of Genoa, in The Treatise).

Clemency Prayer

O my God, I recommend to Thy clemency the holy souls in purgatory, and especially those to whom I am most indebted by the bond of charity or of justice; and chiefly implore Thee in behalf of those who, during their life, have been most devout to the Blessed Sacrament; as also those who have most loved the Blessed Virgin. For this I offer Thee, my good Jesus, Thy wounds, Thy agony, Thy death, and all the merits of Thy most bitter passion. I know that it is Thy pleasure that I should pray for these holy souls, who are so worthy of Thy love. Hear, then, dear Lord, and grant this my prayer in their behalf, which I present to Thee. Amen.

O Blessed Purgatory!
(The late C. S. Lewis, well-known Anglican author, wrote the following about purgatory.)

Our souls *demand* purgatory, don't they? Would it not break the heart if God said to us, "It is true, my son, that your breath smells and your rags drip with mud and slime, but we are charitable here and no one will upbraid you with these things, or draw away from you. Enter into joy"? Should we not reply, "With submission, Sir, and if there is no objection, I'd rather be *cleansed* first." "It may hurt, you know." "Even so, Sir."

> *"The Holy Sacrifice of the Mass, the Perpetual Sacrifice, is the greatest of all suffrages for the holy souls" (From the Council of Trent).*

"The practice of offering up the Holy Sacrifice for the suffering souls in purgatory comes down to us from the earliest Christian times, and Holy Mother Church has ever laid much stress upon this pious and charitable custom."

Very ancient, too, is the usage of Mass offered on the third (representing the Resurrection of our Lord on the third day), seventh (eternal Sabbath or rest of the holy dead), and thirtieth days (number of days the Israelites mourned for Moses) after the death or burial. It was this celebration on the thirtieth day that became known as "Month's Mind" or in a sense an "ardent desire" to do this or that act for someone.

Pope St. Gregory the Great popularized the pious practice of offering thirty consecutive Masses for *one deceased person*, which are now commonly called "Gregorian Masses." The hallowed tradition has been declared a "pious and reasonable belief of the faithful" on the authority of the Sacred Roman Congregation on Indulgences. One can have these Masses arranged for a deceased soul. Also, you can stipulate in your will to have these Masses offered for yourself. (Please contact your local Diocesan Missions Office.)

With regard to the matter of having Masses offered for the welfare of our souls while we are still alive, and the Masses, which will be said for us after our death, St. Anselm tells us that those which we hear or have offered during life are more profitable than those said for us after death.

"A candle placed before us gives more light than ten candles placed behind us!" (An old proverb).

Eucharistic Prayer II

(This ancient Eucharistic Prayer, which
is found in the Roman Canon, dates
back to the third century. It is repeated
almost verbatim in our Mass today.)

Remember our brothers and sisters who have
gone to their rest in the hope of rising again; bring
them and all the departed into the light of your
presence.

---

*"Aspire to God," says St. Francis of Sales,
"with short but frequent outpourings of the
heart." It is good to pray short indulgenced sighs
of prayer during the day, and especially during
the elevation of the Precious Body and Blood at
Holy Mass on behalf of the holy souls. They are
a language of unspoken sighs of love understood
by the God of Love. "Have pity on us, at least
you my friend," they cry! Watch and wait with
them.*

Aspirations of the Heart

Eternal Father, we offer Thee the Blood, Passion, and Death of Jesus Christ, the sorrows of the
most Holy Mary, and St. Joseph, in payment of our
sins, in suffrage for the holy souls in purgatory, for

the wants of our Mother the Church, and for the conversion of sinners.

Heart of Jesus, burning with love of us, set our hearts on fire for love of Thee.

Divine Heart of Jesus, convert sinners, save the dying, and deliver the souls in purgatory.

Jesus, meek and humble of heart, make my heart like unto Thine.

Sweetest Jesus, be not my Judge but my Savior.

Praised and blessed at every moment be the most holy and divine Sacrament.

Sacred Heart of Jesus, have mercy on me.

My Jesus, mercy!

In Thee, O Lord, do I put my trust; let me never be confounded; deliver me in Thy Justice.

Jesus, Mary, and Joseph, I give you my heart and my soul!

Jesus, Mary, and Joseph, assist me in my last agony!

Jesus, Mary, and Joseph, may I breathe forth my soul in peace with you! Amen.

O Good Shepherd, true Bread, O Jesus, have mercy on us!

Sweetest Jesus, may my heart be a burning lamp of love before Thy altar.

Our Lady of the Most Blessed Sacrament, Mother and Model of Adorers, pray for us who have recourse to thee!

Prayer of St. Francis
(St. Francis said this prayer
before the crucifix in San Damiano.)

All-highest, glorious God, cast your light into the darkness of my heart.

Give me right faith, firm hope, perfect charity, and profound humility, with wisdom and perfection, O Lord, so that I may do what is your holy will. Amen.

Prayer Book of Bishop Serapion of Thmuis
(In the early centuries, throughout both East and West the names of the dead were inscribed on special lists [diptychs], which were recited aloud during the Liturgy. Prayer was made "that the glory of those who are of greater merit may be augmented in heaven and the account of those who are less worthy may be lightened in His secret judgments." This is an ancient, popular prayer.)

We intercede on behalf of all who have fallen asleep of whom memory is made.

After recitation of the names:

Sanctify these souls, for Thou knowest all. Sanctify all these souls which have fallen asleep in the Lord and number them with all Thy holy powers, and give unto them a place and mansion in Thy Kingdom.

O God, who hast authority of life and death, God of the spirits and Master of all flesh, God who kills and makes alive, who brings down to the gates of hell and brings up, who creates the spirit of man within him and takes to Thyself the souls of the saints and gives rest, who alters and changes and transforms Thy creatures, as is right and expedient, being Thyself alone incorruptible, unalterable, and eternal, we beseech Thee for the repose and rest of this servant; give rest to his soul, his spirit, in green places, in chambers of rest with Abraham and Isaac and Jacob and all Thy saints: and raise up his body on the day which Thou hast ordained according to Thy promises which cannot lie that Thou mayest render to it also the heritage of which is worthy of Thy holy pastures.

Remember not his transgressions and sins and cause his going forth to be peaceable and blessed. Heal the grief of his relatives who survive him with the spirit of consolation and grant unto us all a good end, through Thy only begotten Son, Jesus Christ, through whom to Thee is the glory and the strength, in the Holy Spirit forever and ever. Amen.

Psalms

Honoring the Dead
(By St. John Chrysostom.)

Will you honor the dead? Do not spend yourselves in unprofitable lamentations: choose rather
to sing Psalms, to give alms, and to lead a holy life.
Do for them that which they would willingly do
for themselves, were they to return again into the
world; and God will accept it at your hands as if it
came from them.

Let us help and commemorate them. If Job's
sons were purified by their Father's sacrifice, why
would we doubt that our offerings for the dead
bring them some consolation? Let us not hesitate
to help those who have died and to offer our prayers
for them.

The Psalms unite the living with the dead.

" 'Get down low enough and you will pray.' It
is what He taught David, 'a contrite and
humble heart Thou wilt not despise.' Always go
to Him with all your sins in your hands; He
won't send you away" (Rev. A. Dignam, S.J.).

Seven Penitential Psalms
Psalms are lamentations and calls for help that
can be placed into the mouths of the holy souls.

Seven Psalms that awaken one's sorrow for
sin have been used by the Church to express re-

pentance for one's personal sins, and the social evils of the community. The sinner entrusts himself to the loving mercy of God.

These Psalms contain sorrowful expressions; the dominant tone in many is full of confidence, hope, and thankfulness. St. Romuald states that the Psalms are the only way to experience truly profound prayer.

St. Augustine during his last illness requested that these Psalms should be copied out and put on the wall beside his bed. The dying saint read them continually, shedding copious tears.

David wrote most of the one hundred fifty Psalms. As you pray these Psalms, pray from the heart like David.

Psalm 6

PRAYER IN ORDEAL

(David, in deep affliction, prays for mitigation of the divine anger. In consideration of God's mercy. His glory. His own repentance. By faith he triumphs over his enemies.)

Anthem: Remember not, O LORD, our offenses, nor those of our parents; nor take vengeance on our sins.

O LORD, rebuke me not in thy anger,
    nor chasten me in thy wrath.

Be gracious to me, O LORD, for I am
  languishing;
  O LORD, heal me, for my bones are
    troubled.
My soul also is sorely troubled.
  But thou, O LORD — how long?
Turn, O LORD, save my life;
  deliver me for the sake of thy steadfast
    love.
For in death there is no remembrance of
  thee;
  in Sheol who can give thee praise?
I am weary with my moaning;
  every night I flood my bed with tears;
  I drench my couch with my weeping.
My eye wastes away because of grief,
  it grows weak because of all my foes.
Depart from me, all you workers of evil;
  for the LORD has heard the sound of my
    weeping.
The LORD has heard my supplication;
  the LORD accepts my prayer.
All my enemies shall be ashamed and sorely
  troubled;
  they shall turn back, and be put to shame
    in a moment.
Say the "Glory be. . . ."

Psalm 32

CANDID ADMISSION OF SIN
(The blessedness of those whose sins are
forgiven. The misery of impenitence.
Confession of sin brings peace. Safety. Joy.)

Blessed is he whose transgression is
  forgiven,
  whose sin is covered.
Blessed is the man to whom the LORD
  imputes no iniquity,
  and in whose spirit there is no deceit.
When I declared not my sin, my body
  wasted away
  through my groaning all day long.
For day and night thy hand was heavy upon
  me;
  my strength was dried up as by the heat of
  summer.
I acknowledged my sin to thee,
  and I did not hide my iniquity;
I said, "I will confess my transgressions to
  the LORD";
  then thou didst forgive the guilt of my sin.
Therefore let every one who is godly offer
  prayer to thee;
at a time of distress, in the rush of great
  waters,
  they shall not reach him.
Thou art a hiding place for me,

thou preservest me from trouble;
thou dost encompass me with deliverance.
I will instruct you and teach you
the way you should go;
I will counsel you with my eye upon you.
Be not like a horse or a mule, without
understanding,
which must be curbed with bit and bridle,
else it will not keep with you.
Many are the pangs of the wicked;
but steadfast love surrounds him who
trusts in the LORD.
Be glad in the LORD, and rejoice, O
righteous,
and shout for joy, all you upright in heart!
Say the "Glory be. . . ."

Psalm 38

PRAYER IN DISTRESS
(David's extreme anguish. He hopes in God.
His resignation and grief. Prayer.)

O LORD, rebuke me not in thy anger,
nor chasten me in thy wrath!
For thy arrows have sunk into me,
and thy hand has come down on me.
There is no soundness in my flesh
because of thy indignation;
there is no health in my bones
because of my sin.

For my iniquities have gone over my head;
  they weigh like a burden too heavy for me.
My wounds grow foul and fester
  because of my foolishness,
I am utterly bowed down and prostrate;
  all the day I go about mourning.
For my loins are filled with burning,
  and there is no soundness in my flesh.
I am utterly spent and crushed;
  I groan because of the tumult of my heart.
LORD, all my longing is known to thee,
  my sighing is not hidden from thee.
My heart throbs, my strength fails me;
  and the light of my eyes — it also has
    gone from me.
My friends and companions stand aloof
  from my plague,
  and my kinsmen stand afar off.
Those who seek my life lay their snares,
  those who seek my hurt speak of ruin,
  and meditate treachery all the day long.
But I am like a deaf man, I do not hear,
  like a dumb man who does not open his
    mouth.
Yea, I am like a man who does not hear,
  and in whose mouth are no rebukes.
But for thee, O LORD, do I wait;
  it is thou, O LORD my God, who wilt
    answer.
For I pray, "Only let them not rejoice over
  me,

who boast against me when my foot
  slips!"
For I am ready to fall,
  and my pain is ever with me.
I confess my iniquity,
I am sorry for my sin.
Those who are my foes without cause are
  mighty,
  and many are those who hate me
    wrongfully.
Those who render me evil for good
  are my adversaries because I follow after
    good.
Do not forsake me, O LORD!
  O my God, be not far from me!
Make haste to help me,
  O LORD, my salvation!
Say the "Glory be. . . ."

Psalm 51

MISERERE

(David prays for the remission of his sins. For
perfect sanctity. Sacrifice without contrition
will not pardon sin.)

Have mercy on me, O God,
  according to thy steadfast love;
  according to thy abundant mercy blot out
    my transgressions.
Wash me thoroughly from my iniquity,

and cleanse me from my sin!
For I know my transgressions,
  and my sin is ever before me.
Against thee, thee only, have I sinned,
  and done that which is evil in thy sight,
so that thou art justified in thy sentence
  and blameless in thy judgment.
Behold, I was brought forth in iniquity,
  and in sin did my mother conceive me.
Behold, thou desirest truth in the inward
    being;
  therefore teach me wisdom in my secret
    heart.
Purge me with hyssop, and I shall be clean;
  wash me, and I shall be whiter than snow.
Fill me with joy and gladness;
  let the bones which thou hast broken
    rejoice.
Hide thy face from my sins,
  and blot out all my iniquities.
Create in me a clean heart, O God,
  and put a new and right spirit within me.
Cast me not away from thy presence,
  and take not thy holy Spirit from me.
Restore to me the joy of thy salvation,
  and uphold me with a willing spirit.
Then I will teach transgressors thy ways,
  and sinners will return to thee.
Deliver me from bloodguiltiness, O God,
  thou God of my salvation,
  and my tongue will sing aloud of thy
    deliverance.

O Lord, open thou my lips,
  and my mouth shall show forth thy praise.
For thou hast no delight in sacrifice;
  were I to give a burnt offering, thou
    wouldst not be pleased.
The sacrifice acceptable to God is a broken
    spirit;
  a broken and contrite heart, O God, thou
    wilt not despise.
Do good to Zion in thy good pleasure;
  rebuild the walls of Jerusalem,
then wilt thou delight in right sacrifices,
  in burnt offerings and whole burnt
    offerings;
  then bulls will be offered on thy altar.
Say the "Glory be. . . ."

Psalm 102

PRAYER IN MISFORTUNE
(The extreme affliction of the Psalmist.
The mercy of God. To be recorded and
praised by future generations. The
unchangeableness of God.)

Hear my prayer, O Lord;
  let my cry come to thee!
Do not hide thy face from me
  in the day of my distress!
Incline thy ear to me;
  answer me speedily in the day when I call!
For my days pass away like smoke,

and my bones burn like a furnace.
My heart is smitten like grass, and withered;
  I forget to eat my bread.
Because of my loud groaning
  my bones cleave to my flesh.
I am like a vulture of the wilderness,
  like an owl of the waste places;
I lie awake,
  I am like a lonely bird on the housetop.
All the day my enemies taunt me,
  those who deride me use my name for a
    curse.
For I eat ashes like bread,
  and mingle tears with my drink,
because of thy indignation and anger;
  for thou hast taken me up and thrown me
    away.
My days are like an evening shadow;
  I wither away like grass.
But thou, O LORD, art enthroned forever;
  thy name endures to all generations.
Thou wilt arise and have pity on Zion;
  it is time to favor her;
  the appointed time has come.
For thy servants hold her stones dear,
  and have pity on her dust.
The nations will fear the name of the
    LORD,
  and all the kings of the earth thy glory.
For the LORD will build up Zion,
  he will appear in his glory;
he will regard the prayer of the destitute,

and will not despise their supplication.
Let this be recorded for a generation to
   come,
  so that a people yet unborn may praise the
    LORD:
that he looked down from his holy height,
  from heaven the LORD looked at the
    earth,
to hear the groans of the prisoners,
  to set free those who were doomed to die;
that men may declare in Zion the name of
   the LORD,
  and in Jerusalem his praise,
when peoples gather together,
  and kingdoms, to worship the LORD.
He has broken my strength in midcourse;
  he has shortened my days.
"O my God," I say, "take me not hence
  in the midst of my days,
thou whose years endure
  throughout all generations!"
Of old thou didst lay the foundation of the
   earth,
  and the heavens are the work of thy hands.
They will perish, but thou dost endure;
  they will all wear out like a garment.
Thou changest them like raiment, and they
   pass away;
  but thou art the same, and thy years have
    no end.
The children of thy servants shall dwell
   secure;

their posterity shall be established before
thee.
Say the "Glory be. . . ."

Psalm 130

DE PROFUNDIS
(The Church uses this in the Liturgy as
her official prayer for the souls in
purgatory. The just, afflicted by their sins,
implore the divine mercy.)

Out of the depth I cry to thee, O LORD!
  LORD, hear my voice!
Let thy ears be attentive
  to the voice of my supplications!
If thou, O LORD, shouldst mark iniquities,
  LORD, who could stand?
But there is forgiveness with thee,
  that thou mayest be feared.
I wait for the LORD, my soul waits,
  and in his word I hope;
my soul waits for the LORD
  more than watchmen for the morning,
  more than watchmen for the morning.
O Israel, hope in the LORD!
  For with the LORD there is steadfast love,
  and with him is plenteous redemption.
And he will redeem Israel
  from all his iniquities.
Say the "Glory be. . . ."

Psalm 143

A HUMBLE ENTREATY
(David prays for favor in judgment. He
represents his distress. He prays for grace,
for deliverance, for sanctification, for
victory over his enemies.)

Hear my prayer, O LORD; give ear to my
  supplications!
  In thy faithfulness answer me, in thy
    righteousness!
Enter not into judgment with thy servant;
  for no man living is righteous before thee.
For the enemy has pursued me;
  he has crushed my life to the ground;
  he has made me sit in darkness like those
    long dead.
Therefore my spirit faints within me;
  my heart within me is appalled.
I remember the days of old,
  I meditate on all that thou hast done;
  I muse on what thy hands have wrought.
I stretch out my hands to thee;
  my soul thirsts for thee like a parched
    land.
Make haste to answer me, O LORD!
  My spirit fails!
Hide not thy face from me,
  lest I be like those who go down to the
    Pit.

Let me hear in the morning of thy steadfast
  love,
  for in thee I put my trust.
Teach me the way I should go,
  for to thee I lift up my soul.
Deliver me, O LORD, from my enemies!
  I have fled to thee for refuge!
Teach me to do thy will,
  for thou art my God!
Let thy good spirit lead me
  on a level path!
For thy name's sake, O LORD, preserve my
  life!
  In thy righteousness bring me out of
    trouble!
And in thy steadfast love cut off my
  enemies,
  and destroy all my adversaries,
  for I am thy servant.
Say the "Glory be. . . ."

Supplications to Mary, Queen of Heaven

Shining Star of the Third Millennium
(By Susan Tassone.)

Theotokos, Mother of God, bearer of the God-Man, shining star of the third millennium, you who protect us under the mantle of your love, pray for all souls who live in this era of renewed faith now and at the hour of our death.

Obtain for us the grace to repent here on earth. For that is as good as the seal of God's pardon. May the souls who come after, pray for us who ushered in this new springtime. Amen.

> *O Christ, Redeemer of all, appeased by the holy prayers of the ever-Blessed Virgin, do thou protect thy servants.*

A Morning Offering for the Holy Souls

O my God, I offer Thee every thought, word, and deed of the day now beginning for the poor souls in purgatory; my rising and lying down, my going out and coming in, my work and recreation, my sorrows and delights, my successes and disappointments, my good fortune and mishaps, my gains and my losses, my pleasures and pains, all that I may do, say, or feel, beseeching Thee that through the infinite merits of the Passion of Thy Divine Son, to which I unite all my works, these poor souls may be speedily released from their dolorous pains to see, love, and enjoy Thee forever. Amen.

Remember us, O Virgin Mother, as you stand in the presence of God, to speak on our behalf.

Heroic Act of Charity to Our Lady

(The Heroic Act was initiated by St. Gertrude. It consists in offering to God, for the relief of the souls in purgatory, all the satisfactory works done during one's life and all the suffrages that shall be offered for one's soul after death. The person renounces in favor of the holy souls all the indulgences he could gain for himself or herself, with the exception of the plenary indulgence at the hour of death that is reserved to the dying person.)

O Mary, Mother of the Church Suffering, grant me the privilege and the grace of being your apostle in helping the souls in purgatory.

To this end, I beg you to unite all my prayers, works, and sufferings with the virtues, expiations, and merits of Jesus and with your own; and thus united apply them according to your will, to alleviate their sufferings.

For the same end I beg you to accept the infinite fruits of all the Masses of which I shall assist, together with all the Masses, prayers, works, and expiations which may be offered for me during my life and after my death.

Only let me assure you, my dear Mother, that I desire to give you all that I can "and more than I can" that you may thus help your beloved children in their exile of suffering.

Mother of Fair Love, grant that my offering may lead me to enter truly and advance continually in the secret paths of divine love. Amen.

The Hail Mary, Adapted for the Souls in Purgatory
(This rarely seen prayer complements
St. Mechtilde's "Our Father.")

Hail Mary! Behold, most merciful Mother, thy poor and sorrowful children who suffer so grievously in the purification of purgatory. We beg thee, for the sake of the great joy which the angelic salutation caused thee, have compassion on them, and send them thy holy angel to bring them also joyful greeting, and to announce to them release from their sufferings.

Full of Grace! Obtain for them grace, mercy, and remission of the great cleansing they now endure.

The Lord is with thee! He will deny thee nothing, but will hear thy prayer and mercifully come to the assistance of these poor souls.

Blessed art thou amongst women! Aye, among all creatures in the whole world! Bless and render happy with thy intercession the poor imprisoned souls, and deliver them from their bonds.

And blessed is the fruit of thy womb, Jesus, Who is the Savior and Redeemer of the whole world, born without pain of thee, a Virgin! O merciful Jesus, blessed fruit of her inviolate virginity! Have mercy on the souls departed! O merciful Mother, hasten to their assistance!

Holy Mary, Mother of God! Wonderful Virgin Mother, *pray for us sinners* and for the souls in purgatory *now* and forever, *and at the hour of our death;* and as thou didst assist the souls departed in their last agony, so assist them now in their grievous suffering, that delivered by thy motherly intercession they may pass from present suffering to everlasting joy, from their anguish and torment, to everlasting rest and glory, and rejoice with thee and the whole heavenly host through all eternity. Amen.

Prayer in Honor of the Seven Joys of Mary for the Faithful Departed

Hail Mary, tried counselor of the apostles! Remember the joy thou experienced in soul and body when the Archangel Gabriel saluted thee and announced to thee the Incarnation of thy divine Son. Through this joy we beseech thee to intercede with God for us sinners and for the souls in purgatory, that they may be delivered and attain to the eternal joy of heaven. Amen.

Our Father . . . Hail Mary . . .

Hail Mary, truthful instructress of the evangelists! Remember the joy thou didst experience in soul and body when without violation of thy holy virginity thou gavest birth at Bethlehem to thy divine Son. Through this thy joy we beseech thee, intercede with God for us sinners and for the souls in purgatory, that they may be delivered and attain to the eternal joy of heaven. Amen.

Our Father . . . Hail Mary . . .

Hail Mary, strong comfortress of the martyrs! Remember the joy thou didst experience in soul and body when the three holy kings made their worthy offerings to thy divine Son and adored Him as their true God. Through this thy joy we beseech thee, intercede with God for us sinners and for the souls in purgatory, that they may be delivered and attained to the eternal joy of heaven. Amen.

Our Father . . . Hail Mary . . .

Hail Mary, wise preceptress of doctors and confessors! Remember the joy thou didst experience in soul and body when after three days, thou didst find thy Son again in the temple. Through this thy joy we beseech thee, intercede with God for us sinners and for the souls in purgatory, that they may be delivered and attain to the eternal joy of heaven. Amen.

Our Father . . . Hail Mary . . .

Hail Mary, most beautiful ornament of all holy women and virgins! Remember the joy thou didst experience in soul and body when on Easter Day, thy divine Son appeared to thee after His glorious resurrection and with filial love greeted and consoled thee. Through this thy joy we beseech thee, intercede with God for us sinners and for the souls in purgatory, that they may be delivered and attain to the eternal joy of heaven. Amen.

Our Father . . . Hail Mary . . .

Hail Mary, shining crown of all the saints of God! Remember the joy thou didst experience in soul and body when thy divine Son of His own power ascended gloriously into heaven in the presence of His beloved disciples. Through this thy joy we beseech thee, intercede with God for us sinners and for the souls in purgatory, that they may be delivered and attain to the eternal joy of heaven. Amen.

Our Father . . . Hail Mary . . .

Hail Mary, most willing helper and consoler of the living and the dead! Remember the joy thou didst experience in soul and body when thy divine Son invited thee to the bliss of heaven, and after thy holy death introduced thy glorious soul and body into heaven, and placed thee above all the choirs of angels. Through this thy joy we beseech thee, intercede with God for us sinners and for the souls in purgatory, that they may be delivered and attain to the eternal joy of heaven. Amen.

Our Father . . . Hail Mary . . .

Precious Blood, delight of the souls!

Litany of the Most Precious Blood

Eternal Father, I offer Thee the Most precious Blood of Jesus Christ in atonement for my sins, and in supplication for the holy souls in purgatory and for the needs of Holy Mother Church.

Lord, have mercy on us!
Christ, have mercy on us!
Lord, have mercy on us!
Christ, hear us!
Christ, graciously hear us!

God, the Father of heaven! *Have mercy on us!*
God, the Son, the Redeemer of the world, *Have mercy on us!*
God, the Holy Spirit, *Have mercy on us!*
Most Precious Blood of my Redeemer, *Cleanse them, O most Precious Blood!*
Blood of the new, eternal Testament . . .
Price of our redemption . . .
Fountain of living waters . . .
Precious ransom of sinners . . .
Pledge of eternal salvation . . .
Sacrifice to eternal justice . . .
Key to the gates of heaven . . .
Purification of our poor souls . . .
Salvation in our misery . . .
Remedy for our wounds . . .
Forgiveness of our sins . . .
Payment of our debts . . .
Remission of our punishment . . .
Source of salvation . . .
Hope of the poor . . .
Nourishment of the weak . . .
Healing balm for the sick . . .
Reconciliation of sinners . . .
Joy of the just . . .
Refuge of all Christians . . .
Admiration of the angels . . .
Consolation of the patriarchs . . .
Expectation of the prophets . . .
Strength of the apostles . . .

Confidence of the martyrs . . .
Justification of confessors . . .
Sanctification of virgins . . .
Refreshment of the suffering souls . . .
Beatitude of all saints . . .
Be merciful, *Spare them, O Jesus!*
Be merciful, *Hear them, O Jesus!*
Amen.

Glorious Mother,
Wrap Us in Your Holiness

To thee, O most holy Virgin, Mary, my Mother, I turn in supplication, and through that sword which pierced thy heart, when thou didst behold thy beloved Son, Jesus Christ, bow down His head and give up His Spirit, I pray and implore thee, with the greatest confidence to help the poor souls in purgatory, and particularly those of which special commemoration hast been made. O Mother of Sorrows, O Queen of Martyrs, for the love of Jesus who died for us upon the cross, do thou with thy powerful prayers give help also to us, who are in danger not only of falling into purgatory, but even of losing ourselves forever. O Mary, our dear Mother, Mother of Grace, Mother of Mercy, have pity on us.

O Eternal Father, through the most precious Blood of Jesus, and through the most bitter dolors of Mary, have pity and mercy upon the holy souls in purgatory. Amen.

Heavenly Lady of Mount Carmel

O most holy Virgin, Our Lady of Mount Carmel, you are the joy of the Church Triumphant, the help for the Church Militant, and the comfort of the Church Suffering. Therefore, extend, we pray you, your merciful glance on those numerous souls who suffer in the fires of purgatory and free them, that they may be admitted to the Beatific Vision of God as soon as possible.

Remember O holy Virgin, to help especially those of my relatives, and those who are most abandoned and devoid of help. O most merciful Virgin, pour the merits of the precious Blood of Jesus on the elect brides of Jesus Christ until they are comforted in the heavenly glories.

And you, holy souls, O elect souls, who can do so much through your prayers to God for us, intercede, therefore, for us and free us from the dangers of body and soul. Protect our families until we have all been granted admission to eternal happiness. Amen.

Prayer to Our Lady of Montligeon

(Among the hills of the French province
of Perche in Normandy stands La
Chapelle Montligeon. In 1878, Father
Buguet was the parish priest. His main
preoccupation was to pray and to ask for
prayers for all the departed souls,
especially the most abandoned ones. The
shrine today attracts pilgrims from all
over the world.)

Our Lady of Liberatrix, have mercy on all our dead brethren, especially those who are more in need of the Lord's mercy. Intercede for those who have left us; may the purifying love of God lead them to full deliverance.

May our prayer, united with the prayer of the whole Church, obtain for them a joy beyond all their desires and bring consolation and relief to our brethren, in their suffering and distress.

Mother of the Church, help us, pilgrims on earth, to make of our life a time for our interior liberation through our passage towards the Resurrection. Cure us of our wounds of heart and soul.

Help us to become witnesses of the Invisible, already seeking the things that the eye cannot see. Grant us the grace of becoming Apostles of Hope, like watchmen awaiting the dawn.

Refuge of sinners and Queen of all Saints, gather us all, one day, in our Father's House for the eternal resurrection! Amen.

Prayer to Our Lady of Pity
(By St. Alphonsus.)

O Lady of Pity, consoler of the afflicted and Mother of all who believe, look mercifully on the poor souls in purgatory who are also your children and more worthy of your pity because of their incapacity to help themselves in the midst of their ineffable sufferings. Pray, dear Co-Redemptrix, intercede for us with the power of your mediation before the throne of divine mercy and in payment for their debt offer up the life, passion, and death of your divine Son, together with your merits and those of all the saints in heaven and the just on earth, so that, with divine justice completely satisfied, they may come into Paradise soon to thank and praise you forever and ever. Amen.

Prayer to Behold the Beatific Vision

Most Holy Mary, Our Lady of Intercession, whose maternal tenderness gathers in one embrace all the souls redeemed by the Precious Blood of your Son, Jesus, we come before your royal throne with sadness in our hearts as we remember those who have gone before us, but also with unlimited confidence in your intercession.

Death, which burst asunder the bonds of earth, has not destroyed the affection that binds us to those who live in the same faith as we do. O Mary, countless souls await with unutterable anxiety the assistance of our prayers, and the merits of our good works in that place of expiation. Urged by the charity of Jesus Christ, we raise our countenance and heart in supplication to you, the compassionate Mother of all believers, in favor of those suffering souls. Make our prayers of good effect, O Mary; obtain for them the power to move the heart of Jesus our Redeemer through your motherly intercession. Let your incomparable holiness supply the defects of our misery, your love make good our slow affection, your power strengthen our weakness.

Grant, O Queen of heaven, that the ardent desire of the souls of the departed to be admitted to the Beatific Vision may soon be satisfied. We pray you, O Mary, especially for the souls of our relatives, of priests, of those who are zealous in honoring you, of those who did good to the souls of others, of those who wept with them and for them and, finally, for the souls of those who are forgotten. Grant that one day, when we are all reunited in heaven, we may be able to rejoice in the possession of God, in the happiness of your dear presence, in the fellowship of all the saints thanking you forever for all the blessings you have obtained for us, O Mother, our unfailing comfort. Amen.

Say the "Hail Mary" and "Eternal Rest" three times.

Prayer in Honor of the Seven Sorrows of Mary for the Faithful Departed

Hail Mary, most humble handmaid of the Blessed Trinity! Remember the sufferings thou didst endure in soul and body when thy beloved Son shed His precious Blood for us on the eighth day after His birth. Through these thy sufferings, we beseech thee, intercede with God for us sinners and for the souls in purgatory, that they may be delivered from all their sufferings.

Holy Mother, pierce me through / in my heart each wound renew / of my Savior crucified.

Our Father . . . Hail Mary . . .

Hail Mary, chosen from all eternity most holy daughter of God the Father! Remember the sufferings thou didst endure in soul and body when thou wert warned to take flight before the wrath of Herod, and to go with the divine Son, an exile from thy country, into the land of Egypt. Through these thy sufferings, we beseech thee, intercede with God for us sinners and for the souls in purgatory, that they may be delivered from all their sufferings.

Holy Mother, pierce me through / in my heart each wound renew / of my Savior crucified.

Our Father . . . Hail Mary . . .

Hail Mary, most worthy Mother of Jesus Christ, the Son of God, remember the sufferings thou didst endure when thou sought thy divine

Son for three days. Through these sufferings, we beseech thee, intercede with God for us sinners and for the souls in purgatory, that they may be delivered from all their sufferings.

Holy Mother, pierce me through / in my heart each wound renew / of my Savior crucified.

Our Father . . . Hail Mary . . .

Hail Mary, most beloved Spouse of the Holy Spirit! Remember the sufferings thou didst endure in soul and body when thy divine Son took leave of thee and foretold to thee that He must suffer death on the cross for the sins of the world. Through these thy sufferings, we beseech thee, intercede with God for us sinners and for the souls in purgatory, that they may be delivered from all their sufferings.

Holy Mother, pierce me through / in my heart each wound renew / of my Savior crucified.

Our Father . . . Hail Mary . . .

Hail Mary, most beautiful Queen of the holy angels! Remember the sufferings thou didst endure in soul and body when thou didst hear that thy divine Son was condemned to death . . . , and when thou didst behold him carrying His cross upon His wounded sacred shoulders to the place of crucifixion. Through these thy sufferings, we beseech thee, intercede with God for us sinners and for the souls in purgatory, that they may be delivered from all their sufferings.

Holy Mother, pierce me through / in my heart each wound renew / of my Savior crucified.

Our Father . . . Hail Mary . . .

Hail Mary, glorious Queen of patriarchs! Remember the sufferings thou didst endure in soul and body when thy divine Son was nailed to the cross, and when thou didst behold him hanging upon the cross in unspeakable pain until He gave up His Spirit. Through these thy sufferings, we beseech thee, intercede with God for us sinners and for the souls in purgatory, that they may be delivered from all their sufferings.

Holy Mother, pierce me through / in my heart each wound renew / of my Savior crucified.

Our Father . . . Hail Mary . . .

Hail Mary, Mother of the Messiah, foretold by the prophets and most anxiously awaited! Remember the sufferings thou didst endure in soul and body when thy divine Son was taken from the cross, laid on thy virginal bosom, and finally deposited in the tomb. Through these thy sufferings, we beseech thee, intercede with God for us and for the souls in purgatory, that they may be delivered from all their sufferings.

Holy Mother, pierce me through / in my heart each wound renew / of my Savior crucified.

Our Father . . . Hail Mary . . .

"Do not fear, because I, the guardian of your soul, which is the noble temple of God, am always with you" (Guardian angel to St. Margaret of Cortona on her deathbed).

To the Queen of Angels!

(The Doctors of the Church teach that the
guardianship of the holy angels over the souls
of men only terminates at the soul's entrance
into heaven. The guardian angel conducts the
soul to the place of expiation and remains
there with it to console and encourage it, and
no doubt also to inspire its friends, who
remain on earth with desires and good works
for its speedy delivery.)

Mary, Queen of Angels, have mercy toward your suffering children in purgatory. Send them your legion of angels to help them.

O glorious St. Michael, St. Gabriel, and St. Raphael! You seraphim and cherubim! You celestial choirs of thrones and dominations! You virtues, powers, and principalities! All you archangels and angels!

We earnestly pray, in the name of God and His most holy Mother, go swiftly and assist our brothers and sisters in purgatory. They undergo great pain. Console and lead them into the glory of heaven! Amen.

*Holy Mary, Our Lady of Deliverance,
pray for us.*

Prayer for the Deliverance of the Holy Souls

Receive, O Lord, thy servant into the place of salvation, which he (she) hopes to obtain through thy mercy. Amen.

Deliver, O Lord, the soul of thy servant from all dangers of hell, and from all pain and tribulation. Amen.

Deliver, O Lord, the soul of thy servant as thou didst deliver Enoch and Elias from the common death of the world. Amen.

Deliver, O Lord, the soul of thy servant as thou didst deliver Noah from the flood. Amen.

Deliver, O Lord, the soul of thy servant as thou didst deliver Abraham from the midst of the Chaldeans. Amen.

Deliver, O Lord, the soul of thy servant as thou didst deliver Lot from being destroyed in the flames of Sodom. Amen.

Deliver, O Lord, the soul of thy servant as thou didst deliver Moses from the hands of Pharaoh, King of Egypt. Amen.

Deliver, O Lord, the soul of thy servant as thou didst deliver Daniel from the lion's den. Amen.

Deliver, O Lord, the soul of thy servant as thou didst deliver the three children from the fiery furnace, and from the hands of an unmerciful king. Amen.

Deliver, O Lord, the soul of thy servant as

thou didst deliver Susanna from her false accusers. Amen.

Deliver, O Lord, the soul of thy servant as thou didst deliver David from the hand of King Saul and Goliath. Amen.

Deliver, O Lord, the soul of thy servant as thou didst deliver Peter and Paul out of prison. Amen.

And finally, as thou didst deliver, O Lord, the blessed virgin and martyr Thecla, from three most cruel torments, so vouchsafe to deliver the soul of this servant, and bring him (her) to share in thy heavenly joys. Amen.

"Christ is the victim which gives solace to the dead" (St. John Chrysostom).

Holy Hour
Prayers

"The Master is there. Everyone go to Him!"
(St. Peter Julian Eymard).

Eucharistic Wisdom
(A quote from Pope John Paul II's
December 2, 1981, address, when he
began the Perpetual Eucharistic
Adoration in a chapel at St. Peter's
Basilica in Rome.)

"The best and surest way and most effective way of establishing *everlasting peace* on the face of the earth is through the power of Perpetual Adoration of the Blessed Sacrament."

"What will convert America and save the world? My answer is prayer. What we need is for every parish to come before Jesus in the Blessed Sacrament in Holy Hours of prayer"
(Mother Teresa of Calcutta).

Holy Hour Offering

My most sweet Jesus, I desire during this hour to "watch and pray" with Thee and by the love of my poor heart to console Thee for the bitter sorrow that overwhelmed Thee in the Garden of

Gethsemane. I desire to forget myself and all that concerns me excepting my sins, the foresight of which caused Thee so much suffering in Thy agony, and as I was a cause of sorrow to Thee then, so now I desire to be to Thee a consolation.

I offer you this hour of prayer for the holy souls, prisoners of purgatory, for whom Thou didst pray, sweat blood, and accept your bitter passion and death. Grant them mercy, Lord, and let our prayers hasten and deepen the process of purification, the growing and adjusting, the journey forward, the yearning and hope which is found in this mystery of redeeming love. I pray for the soul of [*name*]. If he (she) has any sins to expiate, let the way be easy, the burden light, and the glory — may that come soon.

Angel of the agony, help me so to pass this holy hour that I may console the Heart of my Jesus and promote His interests throughout the world. Merciful Jesus, hear us as we pray for the Church which awaits. Amen.

"Believe, and grieve, and hope. Thank, love, adore, show my soul's wounds, and holy gifts implore" (Father Matthew Russell, S. J.).

Prayer to the Sacred Heart of Jesus
(By St. Gertrude.)

My Good God! I now consecrate and offer to Thy greater glory, every thought, word, action, pain, and suffering, the pulsations of my heart, and the motions of my senses, not only of this day, but all the days of my life; in union with the actions, and Passion and death of Jesus Christ, and His Sacred Humanity in heaven; in union with Masses that have been said, are being said, and will be said to the end of time, throughout Christendom; in union with Jesus in the Blessed Sacrament in all the Tabernacles throughout the world. I offer them for the intentions of the Sacred Heart of Jesus, and for the relief of the suffering souls in purgatory. Amen.

May the Heart of Jesus, in the Most Blessed Sacrament, be praised, adored, and loved with grateful affection, at every moment, in all the tabernacles of the world, even until the end of time. Amen.

Eucharistic God
(By Pope Pius XII.)

The Church in the course of the centuries has introduced various forms of the Eucharist worship which are ever increasing in beauty and helpfulness; as, for example, visits of devotion to the tabernacles, even every day; Benediction of the Blessed Sacrament; solemn processions, especially at the time of Eucharistic Congresses, which pass through cities and villages; and adoration of the Blessed Sacrament publicly exposed. . . . These exercises of piety have brought a wonderful increase in faith and supernatural life to the Church militant upon earth and they are re-echoed to a certain extent by the Church triumphant in heaven, which sings continually a hymn of praise to God and to the Lamb "Who was slain."

Prayer is heard everywhere, yet nowhere is prayer so powerful to God as in the presence of the Blessed Sacrament.

Purgatory and the Blessed Sacrament: A Reflection

(Excerpted from *Blessed Sacrament Book*,
Benziger Brothers, 1918.)

Out of the depths they call to us *"Miseremini!"*
"Have pity on us!"

November brings two sad remembrances —
the pitiable state of the holy souls in purgatory,
they are incapable of helping themselves, and the
abandoned state of our divine Lord on the altars;
and these two are most closely intertwined. It is at
His sacrifice we assist for them; it is He whom we
receive when we want to be heard for the sake of
those who groan amidst the expiatory pain of purification, and who await there the hour of their
deliverance.

It is the adorable Lord that takes to the suffering souls our prayers, good works, and indulgences;
it is this sacramental mediator who receives our
aspirations and makes them fruitful for the poor
captives. Let us then, when we look to purgatory,
view it through the medium of the Blessed Sacrament; that we may obtain a fuller abundance of
light, consolation, and graces for these holy souls.
Oh, it can do a great deal — a visit well made, or a
Mass well heard, or a Holy Communion devoutly
received. We may imagine them with upraised arms
crying to us: "Oh, friends, how we long and yearn
and sigh for union with Jesus in heaven. Oh, do

think of us! Pay a visit for us; assist at holy Mass; give us your holy hour; offer your communion for us; have the adorable sacrifice offered for us — and heaven will bless you a hundredfold!"

Let us listen to their plaintive language, and let us multiply our visits, our Masses, and our Holy Communions. The recording angel will take account of it all; and in the measure we give, in the same will it be meted out to us.

Final Penance

("The souls in purgatory are totally immersed
in the Passion of Christ; this is the way they
are purified" — François Charmot, S.J.)

Lord Jesus, crucified in the presence of your most precious holy Mother, I beg you:

By Thy crowning of thorns and Thy clotted hair give me a true contrition for the sins of my head, my sins of thought.

By Thy bloodstained and clotted hair, pardon the sinful vanity of my hair.

By Thy sacred eyes closed in death, and the tears they shed in life, give me true contrition for the sins of my eyes.

By Thy sacred ears, give me true contrition for the sins of my ears.

By Thy sacred mouth, dried up and parched, I beg you, Lord Jesus, in Thy holy Mother's presence, give me true contrition for the sins of my tongue. Give me true contrition for all the sins of the palate in eating and drinking.

Give me also, for Thy Mother's sake, hearty sorrow for want of fervor, for all negligence when Thy Blessed Sacrament has been on my tongue.

By Thy sacred lips, cold in death, and livid, forgive also, Lord Jesus, every sin of my lips.

By Thy holy face, disfigured with wounds, dirt, and spittle, forgive me all my sins of vanity, and all evil desires to attract undue attention and admiration.

By Thy sacred feet, nailed to the cross powerless in death, grant me a true contrition for my sinful footsteps hastening to do wrong.

By Thy sacred hands, nailed to the cross, cold and motionless, give me a true contrition for all the sins of my hands.

By Thy sacred side pierced and by Thy broken heart, I beg you, in Thy Holy Mother's presence, give me a true contrition for all the sins of my heart.

By Thy wounds, bruises, and swelling sores all over Thy sacred body, from the soles of your feet to the crown of your head, I beg you, in the presence of Thy most sorrowful Mother, grant me a true contrition for all the wickedness of my sinful flesh.

By Thy deep wounds all over Thy body, give me also a true contrition for all my relapses into sin. For as the last lash deepened each wound, so have I by my relapses aggravated each wound.

By Thy Blessed Mother and Thy sacred passion, doubled and trebled by her sorrow, give me true contrition for my sins — the sins I have occasioned in others, my parents, my brothers and sisters, my companions in youth; those with whom I have dealt with in years, some older, some younger; some above me, some below; some now dead, some still living. . . .

Have mercy upon me, O God, according to Thy great mercy; and according to the multitude of Thy tender mercies blot out my iniquity.

From my hidden sins cleanse me, and from the sins of others spare your servant.

Give me grace, O God, my Lord, that I may repay fourfold all whom I have wronged. Amen.

Place of Light and Peace

O gentlest Heart of Jesus,
    ever present in the Blessed Sacrament,
    ever consumed with burning love
    for the poor captive souls in purgatory,
    have mercy on their souls.
Be not severe in Your judgments,
    but let some drops
    of your precious Blood
    fall upon the devouring flames.
And, O most merciful Savior,
    send Your angels to conduct them
    to a place of light and peace. Amen.

St. Mechtilde's 'Our Father'

(On one occasion when St. Mechtilde had
received Holy Communion for the departed,
Our Lord appeared to her, saying: "Recite
for them an Our Father." The saint
understood that she was to recite the prayer
in the following manner. After she had done
so, she saw a great multitude of the souls
ascending into heaven.)

Our Father who art in heaven. I beg of Thee,
loving Father, to pardon the souls in purgatory for
not having worshiped Thee as they ought, but for
having shut their hearts to Thee who didst desire
to dwell there. To atone for their fault, I offer Thee
the love and honor Thy cherished Son rendered
Thee while on earth and the abundant satisfaction
by which He paid the debt of all their sins.

Hallowed be Thy Name. I beg of Thee, O loving Father, deign to pardon the souls in purgatory
for not having worthily honored Thy holy Name,
for having seldom invoked it with devotion, for
having often used it in vain and for having by their
disgraceful lives rendered themselves unworthy of
the name of Christian. In satisfaction for their sins,
I offer Thee the perfect holiness of Thy Son by
which He exalted Thy Name when preaching and
in all His holy works.

Thy Kingdom come. I beg of Thee, O loving
Father, to pardon the souls in purgatory for not
having fervently desired nor carefully sought after

Thy kingdom, in which alone true rest and eternal glory consist. To expiate all the indifference which they have shown for every sort of good, I offer Thee the holy desires by which Thy Son wished us to be the co-heirs of His kingdom.

Thy will be done on earth, as it is in heaven. I beg of Thee, O loving Father, deign to pardon the souls in purgatory, and especially the souls of religious who during life preferred their will to Thine, for not having in all things loved Thy will, and for often living and acting according to their own. To make reparation for their disobedience, I offer Thee the union of the Humble Heart of Thy Son with Thy holy will as also the ready obedience with which He obeyed Thee even unto the death of the Cross.

Give us this day our daily bread. I beg of Thee, O loving Father, to pardon the souls in purgatory for not having received the most holy Sacrament of the Altar with the desire, the devotion, and love which It merits, for having rendered themselves unworthy of It, or seldom or never having received It. To expiate these sins, I offer Thee the perfect holiness and the devotion and love of Thy Son, as also the ardent love and ineffable desire which made Him give us this precious treasure.

And forgive us our trespasses, as we forgive those that trespass against us. I beg of Thee, O loving Father, to forgive the souls in purgatory the mortal sins into which they fell, especially in not forgiving those who offended them, and for not loving their enemies. For these sins, I offer Thee the loving prayer Thy Son made upon the Cross for His enemies.

And lead us not into temptation. I beg of Thee, O loving Father, to forgive the souls in purgatory for not having overcome their vices and concupiscences, for having consented to the temptations of the devil and the flesh, and for having willfully given way to bad actions. To expiate these sins, I offer Thee the glorious victory by which Thy Son overcame the world and the devil, as also His most holy life with its works and fatigues, and His bitter Passion and Death.

But deliver us and them *from* every *evil* and every woe through the merits of Thy beloved Son, and bring us to the kingdom of Thy glory, which is none other than Thy most glorious Self. Amen.

"And may the vision of your beauty be my death" (St. John of the Cross, *in* Spiritual Canticle).

Offering in Honor of the Holy Face
(Adapted from *Purgatory,*
D. J. Sadlier and Company, 1886.)

The holy souls are ever saying and beseeching: "Lord, show us your Face!" They long to see His Face again. This is their *greatest* suffering!

Let us pray:

To Mary, Mother most merciful, who before all others, saw the Face of Jesus in His twofold nativity in Bethlehem, and from the tomb, to plead for those holy souls.

To St. Joseph, who saw the Face of Jesus in Bethlehem and Nazareth.

To the glorious St. Michael, Our Lady's regent in purgatory, one of the seven who stand before the throne and Face of God, who has been appointed to receive souls after death, and is the special consoler and advocate of the holy souls.

To St. Peter to whom Christ gave the keys of the kingdom. To whom Jesus turned His holy Face when Peter denied Him three times. His divine look wounded the heart of Peter with repentant sorrow and love.

To St. James and St. John, who saw the glory of the Face of Jesus on Mt. Tabor and its sorrow in Gethsemane when underneath the olive trees it was covered with confusion and bathed in a bloody sweat for our sins.

To St. Mary Magdalene, who saw the holy Face in agony on the cross, when its incomparable beauty was obscured under the sins of the world, and who assisted the Virgin Mary to wash, anoint, and veil the bruised, pale features of her Divine Son.

To the Virgin Martyrs because of their purity, love, and sufferings they endured to see in heaven the Face of their King. Amen.

"Eternal Father, since you have given me for my inheritance the adorable Face of your adorable Divine Son, I offer that Face to you. I beg you, in exchange for this coin of infinite value, to forget the ingratitude of souls dedicated to you and to pardon all poor sinners. Amen" (St. Thérèse of Lisieux, Doctor of the Church).

Short Litany with the Angel of the Agony
(By Ven. John Henry Newman.)

Jesu! by that shuddering dread which fell on Thee;

Jesu! by that cold dismay which sickened Thee;

Jesu! by that pang of heart which thrilled in Thee;

Jesu! by that mount of sins which crippled Thee;

Jesu! by that sense of guilt which stifled Thee;

Jesu! by that innocence which girdled Thee;

Jesu! by that sanctity which reigned in Thee;

Jesu! by that Godhead which was one with Thee;

Jesu! spare those souls which are so dear to Thee;

Who in prison, calm and patient, wait for Thee;

Hasten, Lord, their hour, and bid them
   come to Thee,
To that glorious Home, where they shall
   ever gaze on Thee.

Eucharistic Whisperings to Jesus

Sweet Jesus, suppose that I really must go to purgatory. Well then, my Jesus, I want to ask You now, while I still have time, for a great grace. You will not say, "No," will You, Jesus? . . . Dear Jesus, You know that I cannot separate myself from You; therefore, should it be that my soul is not all pure when it appears before You in eternity . . . should You first have to send me away again until the stains upon my soul have been wholly blotted out and my punishment undergone . . . O then let me at least atone near Your Tabernacle. . . .

If I still have faults to weep over, let me shed my tears here in Your Temple . . . let my complaints be here mingled with the sacred songs that arise to You . . . let my pleadings be united with the prayers that go up to You in heaven from the altar here. . . . Should it be that I must experience the severity of Your justice for a long, long time — *fiat* — let it be done! Only grant that it may be done in the Tabernacle shadow . . . in the shadow of Your sweet Heart, my Jesus.

This, then, is the grace I beg of You, Savior

mine. And yet I would like it better still if You would let me become holy during my lifetime. Otherwise, make me holy after my death there where I know I am near to You.

The Psalter of Jesus

(There are three sorts of psalters: The first is
David's, which contains one hundred fifty
Psalms; the second, our Blessed Lady's, is
composed of one hundred fifty Ave's; the third
is the *Psalter of Jesus*, containing fifteen
petitions. An English Carthusian Father in the
fifteenth century composed the "Jesus psalter."
It was a very popular devotion. Here we have
the tenth petition.)

Jesus, Jesus, Jesus, send us here our purgatory. Jesus, Jesus, Jesus, send us here our purgatory. Jesus, Jesus, Jesus, send us here our purgatory.

Jesus, send us here our purgatory, and so prevent the torments of that cleansing fire which awaits those souls in the next world that have not been sufficiently cleansed in this.

Vouchsafe to grant us those merciful crosses and afflictions that you see necessary for taking off our affections from all things here below.

Since none can see you who love anything that is opposed to your will, suffer not our hearts to find any rest here but in sighing after you.

Too bitter, alas! will be the anguish of a soul

that is separated from you, which desires, but unable to come to you, being bound with the heavy chains of sin.

Here then, O my Savior, keep us continually mortified to this world, that being purified thoroughly by the fire of your love, we may immediately pass from here into your everlasting embrace.

Have mercy on the souls in purgatory, for your bitter passion, we beseech you, and for your glorious name, Jesus. Amen.

'Come Away with Me and Rest Awhile'

Voice of our soul. We thank you, Lord, for that inevitable ordeal — death; it renders without pity all beings.... Cold and unstoppable it tears from us all those you have confided to our love.... Recall your sadness, Jesus, as you drew near the house in Bethany where your friend, Lazarus, no longer awaited you; happily, Jesus, the source of those tears you shed over the death of the friend of our heart is not yet dried up.... Yes, your divinely beautiful eyes still seem wet with the tears of the Man-God who wished to love with all the emotions and tenderness as well as with all the weakness of our heart of flesh.... And this, Jesus, is you present in the Host, whom we adore here, on our knees....

Look at us from the depths of the Tabernacle, and look at those who no longer walk with us along the way; they were like the very fibers of our heart. . . . Now they are gone from us; they have left us. . . . What separation is as cruel as the separation of Death!

You wept at the tomb of Lazarus though you knew you were about to raise him from the dead. . . . Likewise, in spite of the lively faith with which we accept the crosses you send us, you allow our souls to be lacerated when we see our dear ones leave, never to return. . . . When we have loved deeply, these wounds can be soothed; but as you well know, Jesus, they can never be healed completely. . . . Jesus, come to fill the empty place which pitiless death has made, with your permission, in our hearts and homes.

Come to give calm and resignation to us who survive that we may pray at their grave. . . . Come, Master, let us pray together for our dead so dearly loved. . . . May the brightness of your eternal light shine on them. . . . May they rest in peace . . . in the heaven of your Heart!

Accept, Lord, as a bouquet of myrrh, the remembrance of our beloved dead. . . . Bless them, for they have left us only in answer to your divine call.

Sacred Heart, sanctify all our sorrows!

Accept the tears of resignation we have shed on the tombs of those dear to us. . . . Remember particularly little children and families in mourning.

Sacred Heart, sanctify all our sorrows!

Come, dearest Savior, to make up for the loss

of our loved ones who have gone before us. They have left an empty place that only you can fill.

Sacred Heart, sanctify all our sorrows!

Voice of the Master. Children of My love, how sweet and consoling this hour has been which you have shown Me the deep hurts, which torture your souls . . . while I have let you penetrate the ever bleeding Wound of My Sacred Heart. . . . Ah! what a happy similarity of suffering! How we resemble each other when we mourn on earth the bitter afflictions of earth! That is how Gethsemane becomes for you, as well as for Me, a sanctuary of prayer and perpetual redemption. . . . Oh! let us love each other, O My friends, that our hearts may meet on the sorrowful way. . . . Let us love each other, O My little children, in the Cross!

Come unto Me, you who are in mourning, who weep the loss of a son, a mother, a spouse, a brother. . . . Come, without delay, to My Tabernacle, all you whose dwelling has been marked by the cross of death and tears. . . .

Come lift up your hearts, for time is only a passing shadow, and heaven is eternal; arise, then, with courage and take the living Bread, My Eucharist, to fortify you in the struggle; come and I will reward you in the Paradise of My Heart which loves you!

Eternal Courts of Heaven

Do pray! Pray for these poorest of the poor. Do it, My child, in order also greatly to comfort My Sacred Heart, to give Me the joy of soon seeing them in My heaven. This beautiful act of Christian charity will bear abundant fruit for you, not only during your earthly sojourn, not only at the hour of your death, but also — and especially — when you yourself must languish in the chastening flames of love. But the richest reward you will get from Me, as soon as you come to heaven.

Scarcely will you have passed through the gates of heaven, when I will hasten to meet you. But I will not be alone; a large number of the blessed will accompany Me.... You will recognize them at a glance; your dear ones will be there, those that you loved so much and mourned so deeply. And with them will be many other souls. They will surround you in grateful love; for you helped them. With your prayers and good works you extinguished the flames that enveloped them.

Their faces will be transfigured and resplendent with glory! Souls bright with the splendor of beauty immortal.

And when are you going to see them again? When will the day break and the shadows flee away? ... My child, that day is nearer than you think! In heaven above, the souls of our dear departed may be preparing for your reception even now ... for you.

Yes . . . yes, the procession that is to receive you is forming even now. . . . The days and the weeks pass so swiftly in the rapture of heaven, you know. A little more patience, My child. . . . Yet a little while upon the cross of your earthly exile . . . and then . . . then heaven's pearly gates will swing open. . . .

So leave inconsolable sorrow to those who have no hope. . . . Let your glance rise above gloomy graves. . . . Let your heart soar aloft . . . up and ever up . . . higher and ever higher . . . to the very stars and beyond . . . up to God and His heaven.

Listen! Do you not already hear the familiar accents, O the sweet voice that so long was as music to you, until death caused it to die away? Hark! It is calling you. . . . It is pleading that you be pious and true, that heaven may surely be yours. . . . To-day it is but a dear sweet voice. . . . And tomorrow? . . . Ah! Tomorrow will bring a dear sweet face . . . and a loving heart . . . and two welcoming arms stretched out to embrace you! . . .

Yes, tomorrow . . . there will be a happy home-coming of the dear ones in the eternal courts of heaven! Forever!

Passion of Our Lord

O most sweet Jesus, through the sweat of blood which you suffered in the garden of Gethsemane, have pity upon the holy souls in purgatory, and in particular upon the one which was most devout to the most Holy Trinity.

Have pity upon them, O Jesus, have pity upon them.

Our Father, Hail Mary, Eternal Rest . . .
O turn to Jesus, Mother! turn,
And call Him by His tenderest names;
Pray for the holy souls that burn
This hour amid the cleansing flames.

O most sweet Jesus, through the torments which you did suffer in your most cruel scourging, have pity upon those dear souls, and particularly upon the one which was the most devout to your most amiable Heart.

Have pity upon them, O Jesus, have pity upon them.

Our Father, Hail Mary, Eternal Rest . . .
O turn to Jesus, etc.

O most sweet Jesus, through the pangs which you did suffer in your most painful crowning with thorns, have pity upon those dear souls, and particularly upon the one which was most devout to the Immaculate Heart of Mary.

Have pity upon them, O Jesus, have pity upon them.

Our Father, Hail Mary, Eternal Rest . . .
O turn to Jesus, etc.

O most sweet Jesus, through the afflictions which you did suffer in carrying the cross to Calvary, have pity upon those dear souls, and particularly upon the one which is nearest to its departure from that most painful prison.

Have pity upon them, O Jesus, have pity upon them.

Our Father, Hail Mary, Eternal Rest . . .

O turn to Jesus, etc.

O most sweet Jesus, through the tortures which you did suffer in your most cruel crucifixion, have pity upon those souls, and especially upon that one you know to be all the most destitute of special suffrages.

Have pity upon them, O Jesus, have pity upon them.

Our Father, Hail Mary, Eternal Rest . . .

O turn to Jesus, etc.

O most sweet Jesus, through the pains which you did suffer in the most bitter agony which you did undergo upon the cross, have pity upon those dear souls, and particularly upon the one which among them all would be the last to depart out of such excruciating pains, worse than any illness or suffering on earth.

Have pity upon them, O Jesus, have pity upon them.

Our Father, Hail Mary, Eternal Rest . . .

O turn to Jesus, etc.

O most sweet Jesus, through that intense anguish which you did suffer, when you breathed out your spirit, have pity upon those dear souls, and particularly upon the one which has the greatest claims on me for help.

Have pity upon them, O Jesus, have pity upon them.

Our Father, Hail Mary, Eternal Rest . . .

O Mary, let thy Son no more
His lingering spouses thus expect:
God's children to their God restore,
and to the Spirit His elect.

They are like the children of thy tears;
then hasten, Mother, to their aid;
In pity think each hour appears
an age while glory is delayed.

Pray, then, as thou hast ever prayed;
angels and souls, all look to thee;
God awaits thy prayers, for He hath made
those prayers His law of charity.

O turn to Jesus, Mother! turn,
And call Him by His tenderest names;
Pray for the holy souls that burn
This hour amid the cleansing flames.

O holy souls, tormented in most cruel pains, as one truly devoted to you I promise never to forget you, and continually to pray to the Most High for your release. I beseech you to respond to this offering which I make to you and obtain for me from God, with whom you are so powerful on behalf of the living, that I may be freed from all dangers of soul and body; I beg both for myself and for my relations and benefactors, friends, and enemies, pardon of our sins, and the grace of per-severance in good, so we may save our souls. Set us free from all misfortunes, miseries, sicknesses, trials, and labors.

Obtain for us peace of heart; assist us in all our actions; help us promptly in all our spiritual and temporal needs; console and defend us in our dangers. Pray for the Supreme Pontiff, for the exaltation of holy Church, for peace between nations, for Christian princes, and for tranquility among peoples; and obtain that we may one day all rejoice together in Paradise forever and ever. Amen.

Prayer of 'The Gaed Gael'
(By R. MacCrocaigh, 1914.)

O King of the Friday
whose limbs on the cross were bound;
O Lord, who did suffer
sharp pain in many a wound;
We lay us to rest
beneath the shield of Thy might,
may fruit from the tree
of Thy Passion fall on us this night.

Devotion to the Five Wounds
on Behalf of the Poor Souls in Purgatory
(The reader is encouraged to precede the
"Devotion to the Five Wounds" with the
following: "Go before our actions, we beg

you, O Lord, with your inspiration, and
follow after them with your help, that every
prayer and work of ours may begin from you
and through you. Amen.")

We offer to you, O eternal Father, Father of
mercies, for those souls so dear to you in purgatory, the most precious Blood shed on Calvary from
the wound in the left foot of Jesus, your Son, our
Savior, and the sorrow of Mary, His most loving
Mother, in beholding it. We pray . . .

*Recite the Divine Mercy Chaplet on ordinary ro-
sary beads.*

We offer to you, O eternal Father, Father of
mercies, for those souls so dear to you in purgatory, the most precious Blood shed on Calvary from
the wound in the right foot of Jesus, your Son, our
Savior, and the sorrow of Mary, His most loving
Mother, in beholding it.

We offer to you, O eternal Father, Father of
mercies, for those souls so dear to you in purgatory, the most precious Blood shed on Calvary from
the wound in the left hand of Jesus, your Son, our
Savior, and the sorrow of Mary, His most loving
Mother, in beholding it.

We offer to you, O eternal Father, Father of
mercies, for those souls so dear to you in purgatory, the most precious Blood shed on Calvary from
the wound in the right hand of Jesus, your Son,
our Savior, and the sorrow of Mary, His most loving Mother, in beholding it.

We offer to you, O eternal Father, Father of

mercies, for those souls so dear to you in purgatory, the most precious Blood shed on Calvary from the pierced side of Jesus, your Son, our Savior, and the sorrow of Mary, His most loving Mother, in beholding it.

Let us pray:

And now, to give greater value to our feeble prayers, turning to you, most loving Jesus, we humbly pray to you to offer yourself to the eternal Father the sacred wounds of your feet, hands, and side, together with your most precious Blood and your agony and death; and Mary, Virgin of Sorrows, present together with the most sorrowful passion of your well beloved Son, the sighs, tears, and all the sorrows suffered by you through His sufferings, so that through their merits the souls who suffer in the most passionate flames of purgatory may obtain refreshment, and freed from this prison torment, may be clothed with glory in heaven, there to sing the mercies of God forever! Amen.

"When you offer my holy wounds for sinners, you must not forget to do so for the souls in purgatory, as there are but few who think of their relief" (Our Lord to Sister Mary Martha Chambon).

Chaplet of the Holy Wounds
(To be prayed using the rosary beads.)

On the crucifix and first three beads:

O Jesus, Divine Redeemer, be merciful to us and to the whole world. Amen.

Strong God, holy God, immortal God, have mercy on us and on the whole world. Amen.

Grace and mercy, O my Jesus, during present dangers; cover us with Thy Precious Blood. Amen.

Eternal Father, grant us mercy through the Blood of Jesus Christ, Thine only Son; grant us, mercy, we beseech Thee. Amen. Amen. Amen.

On the large beads:

Eternal Father, I offer Thee the wounds of our Lord Jesus Christ.

To heal the wounds of our souls.

On the small beads:

My Jesus, pardon and mercy.

Through the merits of Thy holy wounds.

Thy Holy Wounds are the treasure of treasures for the souls in purgatory.

An Invocation to the Most Holy Trinity for the Souls in Purgatory

O God, all goodness, Father of mercies, Who, at the prayers and fastings of your faithful people, did vouchsafe to send your angels to break the chains of your holy apostle Peter, and to open the doors of his prison; hear even also on this day the prayers and supplications of your Church, and send your angel to the souls for whom we pray, that, the doors of their prison being opened wide, they may be happily received into the bosom of your mercy.

Our Father . . . Hail Mary . . . Glory be . . .

O Son of God, Savior of souls, Who refreshed the three children in the fiery furnace, pour down upon the souls that cry to you from the flames, your heavenly dew. Your precious blood alone can quench the flames of purgatory; oh, let it now flow down upon these suffering souls and do Thou, O Lord, have mercy upon them.

Our Father . . . Hail Mary . . . Glory be . . .

O Spirit of love, have compassion on the cruel torment which these souls endure, that are filled with the purest charity, and, aspiring without ceasing towards their God, cry aloud in their distress, "I thirst, I thirst after my God!" — and yet cannot attain unto the object of their love, nor receive the least drop of that torrent of pure delights. O Holy Spirit, grant that, having felt the fiercest pangs of love, they may taste its heavenly delights in a blessed eternity. Amen.

Our Father . . . Hail Mary . . . Glory be . . .

Prayer at the End of the Visit

O Lord Jesus, I give Thee thanks for the graces Thou didst bestow upon me in this sanctuary. I offer Thee this visit in union with Thy most holy prayers, and I ask Thee to offer them for me to Thy eternal Father. Repair all my negligences and help me to amend my life.

Listen favorably to all my requests, O Jesus, and bless them; grant me an ardent love for the Blessed Eucharist. Grant that in all places my heart may be inflamed with love for the Blessed Sacrament, preferring the hour spent at Thy feet above all other hours of the day. Dispose me better for the worthy reception of Holy Communion, and increase in me the desire of honoring Thee and of causing others to love and honor Thee in the Blessed Sacrament.

I commend to Thee the needs of my soul, the needs of my family and of my friends. Help holy Mother Church, the Sovereign Pontiff, bishops, priests, religious, and all the faithful. Direct all labors of the apostolic missionaries; convert all infidels, heretics, and sinners; bring them to repentance.

Grant the grace of a happy death to all who are now in their agony; have pity on the holy souls suffering in purgatory and release them. O my Jesus, grant me the grace of final perseverance and fidelity in asking for it every day. Deliver me from a sudden and unprovided death.

Bless me, O Lord, as Thou didst bless the little children who were brought to Thee; as Thou didst bless Thy disciples, at Thy glorious Ascension into heaven, so that I may persevere in Thy grace and be numbered on the last day among the elect, who Thou wilt call the blessed of Thy Father, and invite into Thy eternal kingdom forever. Amen.

Invoking the
Saintly Ones

All Souls

(By St. Augustine of Hippo,
Father of the Church.)

It is inevitable that we should be sad when those we love depart from us by dying. Although we know they are not leaving us, for that they have but gone a little ahead of us, that who remain will follow them, nevertheless our nature shrinks from death, and when it takes a loved one we are filled with sorrow simply because of our love for that person. That is why the apostle did not tell us that we should not be saddened, but that we should not be saddened in the same way as those who have no hope. The death of those who are close to us we experience a sadness at the necessity of losing them, and hope of getting them back. By the former we are distressed, the latter consoled; in the one our weakness touches us, in the other faith restores us. In our loss the human condition mourns, but through hope the divine promise heals.

May the angels lead us into Paradise; may the martyrs come to welcome us and lead us into the holy city of Jerusalem.

To Our Patron Saint

O great saint, whose name I bear, protect me, pray for me, and intercede for me that I may avoid purgatory.

Teach me, like you, to love my neighbor, forgive everyone, and do God's will in all things.

Then, one day, may I join you in heaven to glorify God forever. Amen.

Ite ad Joseph ('Go to Joseph')

O Great St. Joseph! Father of the Third Millennium! Who loved so tenderly Jesus, and who have felt so fiercely the rigors of His absence during the time that you were in Limbo.

I recommend vividly the soul of [*name*], who perhaps is suffering at this moment in purgatory.

Be his (her) consoler in this place of grief and expiation. Please favor him (her) with pious suffrages of the faithful and in particular those offered to Jesus and Mary. And by your prayers deliver the bonds that hold him captive so that he (she) can be released into the bosom of God and inebriate eternally the torrents of delight. Amen.

Prayer to St. Nicholas of Tolentino

(St. Nicholas is honored as one
of the patrons of the holy souls.)

O glorious St. Nicholas of Tolentino, in whose prayers the suffering souls had such faith they revealed to you the pains of purgatory, and did implore thee to offer the Holy Sacrifice that the flames might be quenched by the Blood of our Lord Jesus; O glory of the Augustinian Order, we beseech thee to pray for us and for the suffering souls, that they may be speedily delivered from the pains which their sins deserve, and that we may one day rejoice with thee and them in heaven. Amen.

Prayer for the Dead

(By St. Alphonsus Liguori.)

My God! I recommend to Thee the souls of my relations, my benefactors, my friends, and my enemies, and of those who are in purgatory on my account.

I recommend to Thee the souls of evangelical laborers, of religious and priests, and especially of those who had charge of my soul.

I recommend to Thee the souls of those who were most devout to the Passion of our Lord, to the Blessed Sacrament, to the Sacred Heart of Jesus, and to the Blessed Virgin Mary, the souls who are most abandoned, those who suffer most, and those who are nearest to the entrance into paradise.

Novena Prayer to
Blessed Mary of Providence

Blessed Mary of Providence, you gave praise and thanks to God through your love and care not only of the living but also toward those who have gone before us.

Help me to grow in this way of life. Take my needs and desires today [*mention them here*] and hear the prayers of those who call on you.

Help us in our endeavors to carry out our resolutions, to lead a prayerful life, to die a good death, and be with one another in eternal happiness. Amen.

Prayer for Mothers
(By St. Augustine of Hippo,
Father of the Church.)

God of my heart, putting aside for a time those good deeds of my mother, for which I joyfully thank Thee, I do now entreat Thee for her sins. By that Medicine of our wounds, who hung upon the tree, and now sits at the right hand to make intercession for us, O hear me. I know that she dealt mercifully with those who trespassed against her. Do Thou forgivest her the trespasses of which she may have been guilty in a life of many years, since the time when she entered the water of salvation. Forgive them, O Lord, forgive them, I beseech Thee: enter not into judgment with her. Let mercy rejoice against judgment, for Thy words are true, and Thou wilt have promised mercy unto the merciful. That they were so, was Thy gift, who will have mercy on whom Thou wilt have mercy, and will have compassion on whom Thou wilt have compassion. And, as I do believe, Thou hath already performed what I ask for. Do accept, O Lord, the freewill offerings of my mouth. Amen.

Churchyard Prayer

(This prayer is by Pope John XXII. An indulgence is granted the Christian faithful who devoutly visit a cemetery and pray, if only mentally, for the dead. This indulgence is applicable only to the souls in purgatory. This indulgence is a plenary one from November 1 through November 8. On other days of the year it is partial.)

Hail, all you faithful souls whose bodies rest here and elsewhere in dust; may Our Lord Jesus Christ, who redeemed you and us with His most precious Blood, vouchsafe to release you from your pains to unite you to the hosts of the angels; and there do you be mindful of us and suppliantly pray for us that we may join your company and be crowned along with you in heaven. Amen.

Prayer for the Feast of the Faithful Departed

(In 998, St. Odilo, abbot of Cluny, established in all the monasteries of his Order the Feast of the Faithful Departed and ordered that the Office be recited for them all. This devotion was approved by the popes and became the Feast of All Souls celebrated on November 2.)

O holy souls, I promise never to forget you, and to pray to the Most High for your release. I beseech you to respond to this offering which I make to you. Obtain for us peace of heart, assist us in all our actions, console and defend us in our dangers that we may one day all rejoice together in Paradise.

O God the Creator and Redeemer of all the faithful, give to the souls of your departed servants the remission of their sins that they may obtain the joys of heaven. We ask this through Christ, Our Lord. Amen.

St. Odilo, patron of the souls in purgatory, pray for us.

Soul's Light

(By Susan Tassone.)

Blessed virgins, who watching continually with your lamps prepared, were ready at the first voice of the chaste Spouse of heaven to enter the Wedding Banquet.

May our hearts be a lamp, the light which will burn and shine for love of the holy souls in purgatory.

Help us to keep vigilant and to pray constantly, filling our oil lamps with prayers for our beloved dead.

Join our weak prayers to yours and place them in the gold of your glory and of your intercession.

Then as the Angel Raphael said to Tobias, *"I offer thy prayers to God,"* let them be as incense rising in God's sight and from there descend like heavenly balm on the holy souls. Amen.

Mortal man, learn wisdom from the dead! Heed the poor souls' warning: "Today is my turn, tomorrow will be yours!"

The Holy Souls Plead

(St. Thomas More wrote this primarily to reply
to the attacks against Masses for the Dead. His
plea reflects a deep and sincere piety in the
name of the neglected souls of the departed.)

And therefore, since we lie so sore in pains
and have in our great necessity so great need of
your help, and that you may so well do it, whereby
also shall rebound upon yourselves an inestimable
profit, let never any slothful oblivion erase us out
of your remembrance, or malicious enemy of ours
cause you to be careless of us, or any greedy mind
upon your goods withdraw your precious alms from
us. Think how soon you shall come here to us;
think what great relief and rebuke would then your
kindness be to you, what comfort on the contrary
part when all we shall thank you, and of what help
you shall have here of your goods sent here.

Remember what kin you and we be together,
what familiar friendship we had between us, what
sweet words you have spoken and what promise
you have made us. Let now your words appear and
your fair promise be kept. Now, dear friends, remember how nature and Christendom bind you
to remember us. If any point of your old favor, any
piece of your old love, any kindness of kindred,
any care of acquaintance, any favor of old friendship, any spark of charity, any tender point of pity,
any regard of nature, any respect of Christendom,
be left in your breasts, let never the malice of a few

fond fellows erase out of your hearts the care of your kindred, regard for your old friends, and all remembrance of all Christian souls.

Remember our thirst while you sit and drink, our hunger while you are feasting, our restless watch while you are sleeping, our sore and grievous pain while you are playing, our hot burning fire while you are in pleasure and sporting. So may God make your offspring ... remember you, so God keep you away or not long here, but bring you shortly to that bliss, to which, for our Lord's love, do you help to bring us and we shall set hand to help you there.

Perpetual Light
(By Ven. John Henry Newman.)

O God of the Spirits of all flesh, O Jesu, Lover of souls, we recommend unto Thee the souls of all those Thy servants, who have departed with the sign of faith and sleep the sleep of peace. We beseech Thee, O Lord and Savior, that as in Thy mercy to them Thou became man, so now Thou wouldst hasten the time, and admit them to Thy presence above. Remember, O Lord, that they are Thy creatures, not made by strange gods, but by Thee, the only Living and True God; for there is no other God but Thou, and none that can equal Thy works. Let their souls rejoice in Thy light, and impute not to them their former iniquities, which they committed through the violence of passion, or the corrupt habits of their fallen nature. For, although they have sinned, yet they always firmly believed in the Father, Son, and Holy Spirit; and before they died, they reconciled themselves to Thee by true contrition and the Sacraments of Thy Church.

O Gracious Lord, we beseech Thee, remember not against them the sins of their youth and their ignorances; but according to Thy great mercy, be mindful of them in Thy heavenly glory. May the heavens be opened to them, and the Angels rejoice with them. May the Archangel St. Michael conduct them to Thee. May Thy holy Angels come forth to meet them, and carry them to the city of the heavenly Jerusalem. May St. Peter, to whom Thou gavest the keys of the kingdom of heaven, receive them. May St. Paul, the vessel of election, stand by them. May St. John, the beloved disciple, who had the revelation of the secrets of heaven, intercede for them. May all the holy Apostles, who received from Thee the power of binding and loosing, pray for them. May all the saints and elect of God, who in this world suffered torments for Thy Name, befriend them; that, being freed from the prison beneath, they may be admitted into the glories of that kingdom, where with the Father and the Holy Spirit Thou livest and reignest one God, world without end.

Come to their assistance, all you Saints of God; gain for them deliverance from their place of purification; meet them, all you Angels; receive these holy souls, and present them before the Lord. Eternal rest give to them, O Lord. And may perpetual light shine upon them.

May they rest in peace. Amen.

Royal Road of the Cross
(This was written by Blessed Mary of
Providence, who founded the
Helpers of the Holy Souls.)

If we enter on the royal road of the Cross, each trial or sorrow will be a station before which we shall kneel to adore the hand of Providence, and the last station on that road will be the gate of heaven.

Who but Jesus can satisfy these hungry hearts of ours, starving as they are for happiness! If we thirst after God, we must thirst for everything that draws us closer to Him.

Let us fight the battles of the Lord for that generosity, which St. Ignatius speaks of, when he tells us to go forward at any cost, in spite of all obstacles, never looking back, each day learning a new lesson of sacrifice, until the desire of sacrifice becomes a burning thirst.

If we want to rouse ourselves to courage, we must look at that little door of the Tabernacle, out of which Jesus comes so lovingly to our hearts.

We say every day in our Office of the Dead: "Sacrifice and oblation Thou wouldst not...." Then I said: "Behold, I come." Yes, let us repeat: "Behold,

I come . . . to work all my life, by prayer, by suffering, and by labor for the deliverance of the souls in purgatory."

Prayer Asking for the Help of the Holy Souls
(By Blessed Mary of Providence.)

Holy suffering souls, who can obtain so many graces for us, remember us in the midst of your sufferings. I will work unceasingly to obtain for you the joys of heaven and I know you will plead for me.

Thoughts of Blessed Mary of Providence

Oh, it is well to cherish an ever-increasing desire to live for God alone! Who but Jesus can satisfy these hungry hearts of ours, starving as they are for happiness?

If we would thirst after God, we must thirst for everything that draws us closer to Him.

The more we give ourselves to Jesus, the more He gives Himself to us; and for the soul to which He gives Himself, Calvary becomes Tabor.

Let us make no other projects than to do God's will.

If the souls in purgatory could exchange places with us, how gladly they would suffer, and how slight our sufferings seem to them!

Fear nothing but not to do perfectly God's will.

Let us never refuse to help anyone if it is in our power to do so; and depend upon it, we can do so much more often than we suppose.

You feel as if you did nothing, knew nothing, and felt nothing. Never mind; the good God will contrive to weave a crown for you out of all the nothings you have offered up for His love.

The Cross is at the foundation of every vocation.

Those who cannot suffer cannot love.

The true spirit of abandonment consists in keeping a tight hand over ourselves, and letting God do with us as He pleases.

We must never say, "My sufferings are too great," because it is not true. God measures exactly the sufferings that we can and must endure for the souls in purgatory.

Personal sanctification is the first step towards apostleship. Before we can follow the martyrs to distant lands, we must vigorously accept daily martyrdom of minute sacrifices.

Let us be docile instruments in God's hands. It is a marvelous mystery of love that He should make us of nothing to accomplish something.

Whenever anything happens, I say to myself, It *has* happened; and so it is God who allowed it to happen. I will not puzzle myself anymore with those two words, "why" and "how."

Oh, let us put on Jesus Christ; let us wear His

livery with joy and love, and thus, clothed, descend continually into purgatory, to give to the poor souls, by our acts, our sufferings, and our prayers, all the hope and consolation expressed by the name of Jesus.

We often make Acts of Faith, Hope, and Charity; but it does not often occur to us to make Acts of Joy. And yet it would be very pleasing to God, if for instance, we sometimes said to Him, "My God, how glad I am that I belong to You!"

The souls in purgatory suffer without a moment's interruption. Their helpers must never cease a moment to assist them. How could we think of rest on earth?

St. Jerome says that when the priest offers Mass for the holy souls in purgatory, they suffer no pain. And after Mass, some souls are released.

Prayers for
Specific People

Conversing with Our Departed Loved Ones
(The following was composed by
Blessed Frédéric Ozanam, founder of the
Society of St. Vincent de Paul.)

I seem to see, gathering about me in a better world, those dear and holy friends who have been with me from my cradle, and who now await me beyond the grave. I have a habit of conversing with them; by their aid, my mind arises more easily towards those invisible regions where God dwells. If God dwelt there alone, we could perhaps forget Him: but when we recall, one after another, the good friends who have preceded us to the grave, we are strongly enticed to follow in their footsteps towards our heavenly home. Blessed by our holy mothers, who first set our feet in the way of holiness — in the way that will lead us to reunion with them, now that they have left us for a better world. . . . As the number of our friends beyond the grave increase with it, and as death breaks, one after another, the bonds of friendship that bind us to earth, our thoughts and our conversation will be more and more in heaven. It is a consolation to those parents who lose their children when but infants, to know that they have little angels watching over them and their family — angels who are their own children.

> *"Be faithful until death,"* says the Lord, *"and I will give you the crown of life."*

Acclamations as Prayers
(Acclamations are an ancient form of prayer. They were used as ejaculatory prayers in the Liturgy and inscribed on tombs. The word "peace" meant the peaceful and eternal friendship of God.)

Jesus Christ, the Lion of the tribe of Judah, the root of David, has conquered. Alleluia! Have mercy on the souls of [*names*]. Amen.

O compassionate Father, Son, and Holy Spirit, have mercy on the souls of [*names*]. Give them the rest you keep for your saints. Amen.

Peace and Rest
(Adapted from *Early Christian Prayers*, Longmans, Green and Co., 1961.)

Peace to them that are gone to God. May they be at peace. Peace be with you. The peace of Christ be with you. They sleep the sleep of peace. May they sleep in peace. May they live in peace. At peace in a place of refreshment. Depart in peace. May they sleep in the peace of the Lord. Live forever at peace. In the peace of sleep. With God in peace.

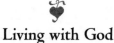

Living with God

May he be with God. May he be with the living God. May he be with the immortal God. May he be in God's hands. May he be where the great name of God is. May he be where God's greatness is. May he be with the living God now and on the day of judgment. Live in God, live in eternal delight.

Lord, this is the people that longs to see your face.

Prayer for Deceased Parent(s)

Dear God, Father of our Savior, incline your ear as I pray for my (father and/or mother) [*mention name(s) here*], whom you have called from this life.

In your most tender mercy, recall (his/her/their) kindness, generosity, love, and devotion to duty. May (he/she/they) attain that Beatific Vision which you have reserved for those who love you and do your will. Amen.

For a Husband or Wife

O Lord of mercy, I pray that you will keep in your care the soul of [*name*], who was my soul mate, companion, and dearest friend in this life.

Grant my beloved your assurance of final salvation in the company of the saints.

May (he/she) join with your choir of heavenly hosts in worship and praise of the Father, Son, and Holy Spirit.

You, dear Lord, brought us together in the Sacrament of Marriage. May the love that we shared on earth find its ultimate meaning in the joy of heaven and our reunion with you. Amen.

For Loved Ones and Friends

O most loving and gracious Savior, I implore your mercy on behalf of the souls of those very dear to me: [*names*].

My God, pour forth your blessings and your mercies upon all persons and upon all souls in purgatory for whom, by reason of charity, gratitude, and friendship, I am bound or desire to pray.

May they now find relief from their temporary suffering through the intercession of this prayer and the benevolence of the saints who already are present to you. Amen.

For a Brother or Sister

I commend you, dear brother (dear sister), to almighty God and commit you to the hand of our Creator, that when by death, you paid the debt of nature, and now may return to our Maker, who formed you from the clay of earth. When your soul leaves the body, may the bright host of Angels come to meet you; the company of the Apostles who are to judge the world receive you; the triumphant army of Martyrs meet you; the multitude of Confessors surround you, with their lilies in their hands; the choir of joyful Virgins welcome you; and may the Patriarchs with loving embrace receive you into their rest. May Jesus appear to you with a mild and radiant face and may He give you a place among those who are ever near Him.

May you never know the dreadful darkness, the crackling flames, and the torments of the damned. May the devil, with his evil spirits, depart from you trembling and flying into the horrid confusion of eternal night, when he sees you accompanied by the Angels. Let God arise, and his enemies be put to flight, and all who hate Him flee before His presence! Let them be driven away as smoke; as wax melts before the fire, so may sinners disappear before His countenance. But may the just rejoice and be glad in the presence of God. Let all the hosts of hell be confounded and put to shame, and may the servants of Satan place no hindrance in your way.

May Christ, who was crucified for you, deliver you from all torments. May Christ, who vowed to die for you, deliver you from eternal death. May Christ, the Son of the living God, conduct you to the possession of the eternal joys of Paradise. May He, the true Shepherd, receive you as His sheep. May He absolve you from all your sins, and place you at His right hand among the number of His elect. May you see, dear brother (dear sister), your Redeemer face to face, and always in His presence behold, with happy eyes, the purest truth. May you, in the company of the blessed, eternally enjoy the sweetest of the Divine Presence. Amen.

They shall be like the angels of God.

For Children

Give me patience, O God, under this trial. It is difficult to nature to be thus deprived of its comfort; but since Thou, O Lord, hast done it, behold, I am silent; I bow down, and say, Lord, Thy holy will, and not mine, be done. This I say with my lips, and I most humbly beseech Thee, to give such a true conformity of spirit, that my heart may go with my words: Lord, Thy will be done. Grant this, O God, that, now at this time, I may join in spirit with Abraham, and offer Thee this sacrifice with the submission of that holy Patriarch.

I must confess, O God, amidst all my uneasiness, Thou hast done as a most loving Father, in taking my child out of this world, in the time of innocence, when there is nothing to obstruct his eternal happiness. For what truer comfort can there be than that my child is now delivered from the infinite dangers of this troubled world, and, without any ever hazard, secured of bliss? Can this be a matter of complaint to a believer? Can it be a subject of grief, that one is arrived safe in the port, and past all danger of storms? Can I pretend to love my child, if at so great an elevation as to be raised from dust to glory, I lament, as if some strange misfortune had befallen him? Don't I see every day the monstrous corruption of this world, enough to believe it a happiness to be taken from it and have it exchanged for bliss?

If my child were now permitted to speak to me, would it not justly reprove my tears, and say: *If you loved me, you would rejoice, because I am gone to the Father.* Would it not turn to me and say, *Weep not for me, but weep for yourselves?* I must confess, O God, there is too much reason for such reproof; for, if I have any true love for my child, I am obliged to rejoice in its happy possession of Thee; and no tears are due to him but all to myself, who am yet in a state of misery, and, after many difficulties and storms, know not whether I shall ever be so happy, or may not be lost eternally.

And is this such a desirable state and that I

should grieve because my child is delivered from it? What if God should, in punishment of my impatience, again replace him here to go through all these hazards? What if, in the hazard, he should miscarry?

No, my God, I know he is well, and my grief is all self-love. But where is the heart of a parent, if I will not bear my loss, for his so great gain? I submit, O blessed Lord; I am unreasonable and blind, and do not understand what is for my good. Help me, therefore, I beseech Thee, to govern my inclinations, to moderate my passion, and teach me, with peace, to submit to my appointments. Now I have an opportunity to make an offering to Thee. Grant, O Lord, I may now do it, and that I may not leave that for time to do, which, by a Christian, ought to be done by strength of reason and faith. Suffer me not, therefore, any longer to be governed by passion or to grieve like an unbeliever; but now, through Thy grace, may I receive Thy orders with cheerfulness and suffer as a Christian. Amen.

For the Newborn, Unborn, or the Miscarried

[*Name*], our (son or daughter), ours for a little while, pray for us. Amen.

For a Child

To you, O Lord, we humbly entrust this child, so precious in your sight. Take him (her) into your arms and welcome him (her) into Paradise, where there will be no sorrow, no weeping nor pain, but the fullness of peace and joy with your Son and the Holy Spirit, forever and ever. Amen.

For a Young Person

Lord God, source and destiny of our lives, in your loving providence you gave us [name] to grow in wisdom, age, and grace. Now you have called him (her) to yourself.

As we grieve the loss of one so young, we seek to understand your purpose.

Draw him (her) to yourself and give him (her) full stature in Christ. May he (she) stand with all the angels and saints, who know your love and praise your saving will.

We ask this through Christ our Lord. Amen.

For an Anniversary Day

O Lord, the God of mercy and pardon, grant to the soul of your servant [name], whose anniversary we commemorate, the seat of refreshment, the happiness of rest, and the brightness of light! Through our Lord Jesus Christ. Amen.

For One's Grandparents

O glorious and good St. Joachim and St. Anne, saints of God's tenderness, who lived in the presence of the Holy Family.

I entrust my grandparents to you. Intercede on their behalf and lead them to Jesus, your beloved Grandson, who is the God of love and everlasting happiness and peace. Amen.

For Family Members
to the Fourth Generation

My dearest Jesus, whose loving Heart was ever touched by the sorrows of others, look with compassion on the souls of our dear ones in purgatory.

O you who "loved your own," hear our cry for mercy and grant that those whom you called from our homes and hearts may soon enjoy everlasting rest in the home of your love in heaven. Amen.

Be mindful, O Lord, of Thy servants who on departing this life were found unfit to enter into Thy joy, and are therefore now being prepared by suffering for that final beatitude. Grant that the claims of Thy justice may be satisfied, and the debts of these helpless sinners be fully paid by their loving Lord and Master, Jesus Christ, the one Mediator of all mankind. Amen.

Prayer to Pity the Dying

O most merciful Jesus, lover of souls, I pray that by the agony of your most Sacred Heart, and by the sorrows of your Immaculate Mother, cleanse in your Precious Blood the sinners of the world who are now in their agony and are about to die this day. Heart of Jesus, once in agony, pity the dying. Amen.

For All: 'Remember Not, O Lord!'

Remember not, O Lord, the sins of his (her) youth, and his (her) ignorance, but according to your great mercy be mindful of him (her) in the brightness of your glory. May the heavens be opened to him (her) and may the angels rejoice in him (her). Receive O Lord, your servant into your kingdom.

May St. Michael the Archangel of God, who has merited to be the chief of the heavenly host, conduct him (her) and take him (her) to the city of the heavenly Jerusalem. May St. Peter, to whom God committed the keys of the kingdom, receive him (her). May St. Paul, who was worthy to be a vessel of election, assist him (her). May St. John, the chosen Apostle of God, to whom the secrets of heaven were revealed, intercede for him (her), that he (she), being delivered from the bonds of the flesh, may merit to be received into the glory of the kingdom of heaven; by the mercy of our Lord Jesus Christ, who with the Father and the Holy Spirit, lives and reigns forever. Amen.

Heavenly Reunions
(By St. Ambrose.)

Since no one, Lord, can desire more for another than he wishes for himself, I ask you not to separate me when I am dead from those who were so dear to me while I lived.

Lord, I beg you that where I am, they too may be with me. As I have not been able to see much of them here, let me enjoy their company in heaven forever.

I beseech you, God most High, to grant a

speedy resurrection to these children whom I love so much. As the span of their life on earth was cut short, make it up to them by calling them sooner to eternal life. Amen.

Dying you destroyed our death, rising you restored our life. Lord Jesus, come in glory! Maranatha! Come, Lord Jesus, for these souls!

Prayer for All Who Died Today

By Thy resurrection from the dead, O Christ, death no longer has dominion over those who died in holiness. So, we beseech Thee, give rest to Thy servants in Thy sanctuary and may my dear patrons smile on me; that in them all, through them all, I may receive the gift of perseverance, die, as I desire to live, in Thy Faith, in Thy Church, in Thy service, and in Thy love. Amen.

For the Pope

O God, from whom the just receive an unfailing reward, grant that your servant [*name*], our Pope, whom you made vicar of Peter and Shepherd of your Church, may rejoice forever in the vision of your glory, for he was a faithful steward here on earth of the mysteries of your forgiveness and grace.

May he be joined forever to the fellowship of your holy pontiffs. We ask this through Christ our Lord. Amen.

For Our Bishop

O God, from the ranks of your priests you chose your servant [*name*], to fulfill the office of bishop.

Grant that he may share in the eternal fellowship of those priests, who, faithful to the teachings of the apostles, dwell in your heavenly kingdom. We ask this through Christ our Lord. Amen.

For a Religious Person

God of blessings, source of all holiness, the voice of your Spirit has drawn countless men and women to follow Jesus Christ and to bind themselves to you with ready will and loving heart.

Look with mercy on [*name*], who sought to fulfill his (her) vows to you, and grant him (her) the reward promised to all good and faithful servants.

May he (she) rejoice in the company of the saints and with them praise you forever. Amen.

For the Clergy
(From the Coptic Liturgy of St. Gregory.)

Remember, O Lord, all those who fell asleep and rested while in the priesthood, and those who were in any order of the laity. Grant a resting place to their souls in the bosom of our fathers Abraham, Isaac, and Jacob; feed them in a green pasture, by the waters of comfort, in the paradise of joy, the place from which the broken heart, sorrow, and sighs flee away, in the light of Thy saints.

Yea, Lord, make them rest in that abode; and us also, who are sojourners in this place. Keep us in Thy faith, and grant us Thy peace unto the end. Amen.

For Our Departed Priests:
'Sleep in Christ'

Gentle Jesus, from the very depths of my heart my cries go out to you today. Gratitude and love compel me to plead at your throne of grace. Accept my heartfelt prayers for the priests who have gone before us with the sign of faith and who now sleep in the sleep of peace.

God of mercy, be mindful of your representatives, who toiled so bravely and unsparingly here below. You saw them at the altar in your churches

. . . saw them in the pulpit and the tribunal of penance . . . saw them labor by word and example — perhaps with tears of which no one knew.

You and your glory and the salvation of souls was their one, all-absorbing thought. How many poor little lambs of the flock were wandering astray on the downward path of destruction, they once brought back to you, following your example, Good Shepherd. . . . How many they kept in innocence pure. . . . How often they dispelled the clouds of ignorance. What consolation they brought to your people cast down by misfortune and adversity. And shall they, after having faithfully fulfilled the duties of their priestly office, after having exhausted the last ounce of energy in their self-sacrificing lives, gentlest Jesus, shall they, despite all this, be compelled to do penance still longer and to suffer in the cleansing flames of purgatory?

O most holy God, you are infinitely good and merciful, but you are also infinitely just. And the rigors of your justice are measured by the exalted dignity to which you raised them, and by the great responsibility incident to their lofty calling, and by the graces that you offered them.

How many a priest I have seen in this church, year after year fulfilling the duties of their sacred office . . . I witnessed their coming and their going. Of these, some venerable figures remain so impressed upon my mind that even today I seem to see them standing here before me. The names of many of these fearless fighters for God and the things of God rise up before me as so many beacon lights of fair example, as models of a truly holy life. And of many, many others with whom I was not personally acquainted I know from hearsay that they did much good. . . .

And must these pious priests now be consigned to that prison house of temporal punishment just because they did not execute their angelic office with the holiness of angels? . . . Dear God, who ever thinks of them? Already in this life, "Thanks" was a rare thing for them; and now that they have gone into the house of their eternity, all feelings of gratitude are forgotten. Alas! How few there are who ever think of praying for departed priests! The number of true and grateful hearts is deplorably small!

Ingratitude and forgetfulness must be hard, very hard, for the poor souls . . . for departed priests they are absolutely crushing.

Poor priests! At every Holy Mass, in their daily Office, year in and year out, they prayed for the faithful departed. . . . And now that they themselves need prayers and good works they are utterly forgotten. . . .

Good Jesus, how you loved them! Each one was the apple of your eye. You made them the privileged recipients of your choicest graces, the custodians of your saving sacramentals, the administrators of your boundless mercy. Oh, show mercy directly to them now, my Savior . . . may they rest in peace.

Pour out your Precious Blood upon them as they languish in purgatorial flames — that Blood which flows without ceasing in the chalices of your priests. Let it fall over their shoulders and clothe them anew with a stole so beautiful that in the eyes of God they may appear immaculate and as white as snow. Here below they sanctified and strengthened our souls with your Precious Blood; now we would offer this Blood to you that they may be refreshed . . . that their poor souls may be freed from the bonds of pain that bind them. O God, deign with one little drop of it to quench the fires of their purgatory . . . to free them from their dark prison.

Kind Savior, when you dwelt among us visibly on earth you had compassion on the poor, the sick, the unfortunate. Everywhere you manifested your power for the relief of pain and sorrow. And, therefore, I beg of you to be mindful of the priests who are in purgatory . . . have mercy on them! Time was when these your representatives had full power over your sacred Body and Blood, over your Soul, over your Divinity and Humanity — over all that you are and all that you have. To them you entrusted the keys of the kingdom of heaven. And now?

Good Master, have these no longer even the power of persuading you to utter one little word of pardon? Good Jesus, reward those who were so unsparing in the care of our souls — give them eternal rest. . . . May they rest in peace!

For these dear departed I offer you your own most holy sufferings — your death — I offer you the Blood that you shed for us ... the Host that radiates in a sea of light in the monstrance here before me ... the Host that is hidden in love's dark prison house of the tabernacle. ... I offer you the Holy Mass that I will hear ... the communion that I will receive, all the indulgences that I can gain today ... the little mortifications that I am going to perform this day for love of You ... the afflictions that your fatherly solicitude will send me. ... I offer you all my good works and the few merits that are mine as well as my poor little prayers, which I am going to unite with the powerful prayers of Holy Mother Church. Today I offer you everything, everything for departed priests, particularly for those who were my pastors and special benefactors.

O Jesus, have mercy on the priest who poured the saving waters of Baptism upon my head and made of me a child of God ... on the priest who instructed me in the truths of my holy faith and who spoke to me of your love. Have mercy on the priest to whom as a child I first entrusted my soul ... who pronounced over me my first confession the *Ego te absolvo* ... who after careful preparation first admitted me to the Holy Table. Have mercy on the priest who later on guided me along the path of virtue ... who welcomed me back, the prodigal son, with all a Father's love ... and like the good Samaritan poured healing oil into the wounds of my soul ... who renewed my zeal and courage and made the service of the Lord light and sweet to me. Have mercy on the good priests for whom I so often made things hard . . . whom I caused so much worry by my indifference and disobedience when they spoke to me of God and of the Church. Have mercy, O Jesus, on all those priests to whom I promised that I would pray for them after their death; for I have not been true to my word — I forgot all about my promise. Have mercy on all those priests who have any special claim on my prayers. My God, deliver them from their sufferings!

Sweetest Savior, when you actually dwell in my heart after Holy Communion, you know best for whom I would really like to pray. I recommend to you the priests who have gone before us. Let them this day be with you in Paradise.

Oh, listen to the voice of gratitude and love that pleads with you in behalf of your ambassadors. Sweet Jesus, summon the souls of departed priests from purgatory to your heavenly throne. Oh, do not delay! Gather them around your own sweet Self in heaven even as on earth they surrounded your Eucharistic abode. To this sublime honor you once called them; and they gladly followed your call. And as here below they were the glory of the altar, so now let them be called to that glorious assembly which forms a wreath round the sublime altar of the spotless Lamb of God. Amen.

For a Deacon

God of mercy, as once you chose seven men of honest repute to serve your Church, so also you chose [*name*] as your servant and deacon.

Grant that he may rejoice in your eternal fellowship with all the heralds of your Gospel, for he was untiring in his ministry here on earth. We ask this through Christ our Lord. Amen.

For One Who Served in Spreading the Gospel

Faithful God, we humbly ask your mercy for your servant [*name*], who worked so generously to spread the Good News; have mercy on those who engaged in apostolic labors, civil rights, in propagating the faith in foreign lands, in giving missions and retreats.

Grant him (her) the reward of his (her) labors and bring him (her) safely to your promised land. Amen.

For the War Dead
(By Pope Pius XII.)

Those who fall in battle deserve to be gratefully remembered. Innocent citizens who were killed are to be counted among the heroes who faced the enemy without weapons. In life they were ready to carry on with quiet bravery, doing the ordinary things necessary for life; dying they did not lose confidence in human government; in death they utter no reproach.

Now some are buried under the pile of rubble of shattered cities; the remains of others are scattered about deserted prison camps. Many of them died in the state of grace, it is true, but suddenly and without the benefit of the Last Sacraments, and with a debt upon their souls.

We could not minister to them and ease their pain while they were dying, but through our prayers we can help now, and obtain for them a speedier release from their sufferings in purgatory.

Divine Redeemer, to your Ascension you preceded us in order to prepare a dwelling with your Father for your followers. We beg you to allow the souls of our departed ones to take possession of this eternal home in peace and blessedness, where sorrow and war and death are forgotten. May your holy angels keep watch at their tombs until resurrection day when you will call their bodies also to glory. You who live and reign eternally. Amen.

For One Who Has Taken His Own Life

(Father Benedict J. Groeschel, C.F.R., in *Arise
From Darkness*, Ignatius Press, 1995. He says:
"The death of a loved one by suicide is one of
the most appalling experiences one can
endure. There is an anguish comprehended
only by those who have experienced it. Since I
lived through a suicide long ago, I write this
prayer just for those who know. Although this
disturbed young man took his life many years
ago, when his girlfriend rejected him, the
gunshot still echoes through my mind.")

Crucified Savior, there is no place for me to
go but to the foot of Your Cross. I feel desolation,
defeat, betrayal, rejection. I tried. I tried to stop the
flood, to calm the earthquake, to put out the rag-
ing fire. I did not even know how desperate it all
was. There is absolutely no consolation, no answer,
no softening of my grief. It is complete darkness. I
grieve for my dear friend [*or relative*], for what was
and what could have been. Is life so awful that all
struggle had to end, that defeat was inevitable? There
is nothing but silence outside and screaming in-
side. I know that the wound will heal, but now I
don't even want it to. I know that there will be a
huge scar in its place. That scar will be all that I
have left.

I am filled with terror for the one I loved and
cared for. Salvation. If only I was certain of salvation for the one who is gone, defeated by this life.

There is no one I can come to but You — Crucified One. Your prayer of dereliction, which always puzzled me before, now is the only thing with any meaning at all. I put my dear one whose body is destroyed into Your hands. Reach down from the Cross and embrace this wounded and broken soul. You descended into hell. Find our friend on the edge and rescue the one who has gone from us. We have no place to go in the world, in the whole universe but here to You, to Your Cross — it is our only hope. Into Your hands, O Lord, we commend this spirit. Amen.

For the Victim of a Violent Death

Lord our God, you are always faithful and quick to show mercy. Our brother (sister) [*name*] was suddenly (violently) taken from us.

Come swiftly to his (her) aid, have mercy on him (her), and comfort his (her) family and friends by the power and protection of the Cross. We ask this through Christ our Lord. Amen.

For Surviving Friends

Grant, O Lord, we implore you, that while we lament the departure of your servant [*name*], we may always remember that we are most certainly to follow him (her). Give us grace to prepare for that last hour by a good and holy life, that we may not be taken unprepared by sudden death, but may be ever on the watch, that when you call, we may go forth to meet the Bridegroom, and enter with Him into glory everlasting.

O most wise and merciful Lord, who has ordained this life as a passage to the future, confining our repentance to the time of our pilgrimage here, and reserving for after this the state of purification and reward; promise to us who are yet alive, and have still the opportunity of reconciliation with you, the grace so to watch over all our actions, and to correct every slightest wandering from the true way to heaven, that we may not be surprised with our sins uncancelled or our duties unfulfilled; but when our bodies shall go down into the grave, our souls may ascend to you, and dwell with you forever in the mansions of eternal bliss. Through Jesus Christ our Lord and only Savior. Amen.

For Non-Christians

Almighty and faithful Creator, all things are of your making, and all people are shaped in your image.

We now entrust the soul of [*name*] to your goodness. In your infinite wisdom and power, work in him (her) your merciful purpose, known to you alone from the beginning of time.

Console the hearts of those who love him (her) in the hope that all who trust in you will find peace and rest in your kingdom. We ask this through Christ our Lord. Amen.

For Our Enemies
(A Celtic blessing.)

This soul did little good to me, O Lord.
But this soul was yours.
So to this soul I say:
I bless the day you were born,
I bless your growing up,
I bless you even in your dark deeds,
And I bless you, soul, at your end.
Travel to God who transforms,
Travel to the Arms so wide,
Travel to the Spirit all generous. Amen.

Early Christians chose their resting places near the tombs of the martyrs. Why? Intercessory prayer. Prayer must rest on suffrages and satisfactions offered by the faithful of the Church Militant. Our Lady, the angels, and saints themselves present these suffrages to God and add to them the weight of their own merit, which increase the value many times over in the eyes of God. Thus, all three members of the Mystical Body manifest themselves in a tangible manner.

Intercession for the Dead

We offer up a Pater and Ave in honor of God and the Virgin Mary for the poor souls who are suffering the pains of purgatory, and especially for the souls of our own relations; for every poor soul for whom there is none to pray; for every soul in great and urgent need; for the souls that have last departed from this world; and for every poor soul burdened with the guilt of an imperfect confession, a forgotten Mass, or a penance not performed. We include them all in this prayer. May God release them tonight. Amen.

Silent Voices
(Karl Rahner, S.J., in *Encounters with Silence*.)

O silent God of those who are silently summoning me to enter into Your life, never let me forget my dead, my living. May my love and faithfulness to them be a pledge of my belief in You, the God of eternal life. Let me not be deaf to the call of their silence, which is the surest and sincerest word of their love. May this word of theirs continue to accompany me, even after they have taken leave of me to enter into You, for thus their love comes all the closer to me. . . . When I pray, "Grant them eternal rest, O Lord, and let Thy perpetual light shine upon them," let my words be only the echo of the prayer of love that they themselves are speaking for me in the silence of eternity. Amen.

Litany of the Faithful Departed

Lord, have mercy on us.

Christ, have mercy on us.

Lord, have mercy on us.

Christ hear us.

Christ, graciously hear us.

God the Father of heaven, *Have mercy on the suffering souls.*

God the Son, Redeemer of the world . . .

God the Holy Spirit . . .

Holy Trinity, one God . . .

Holy Mary, *Pray for the suffering souls.*

Holy Mother of God . . .

Holy Virgin of virgins . . .

St. Michael . . .

All ye holy Angels and Archangels . . .

All ye choirs of celestial Spirits . . .

St. John the Baptist . . .

St. Joseph . . .

All ye holy Patriarchs and Prophets . . .

St. Peter . . .

St. Paul . . .

St. John . . .

All ye holy Apostles and Evangelists . . .

St. Stephen . . .
St. Lawrence . . .
All ye holy Martyrs . . .
St. Gregory . . .
St. Ambrose . . .
St. Augustine . . .
St. Jerome . . .
All ye holy Pontiffs and Confessors . . .
All ye holy Doctors . . .
All ye holy Priests and Levites . . .
All ye holy Monks and Hermits . . .
St. Mary Magdalen . . .
St. Catherine . . .
St. Barbara . . .
All ye holy Virgins and Widows . . .
All ye Saints of God . . .
Be merciful unto them.
Pardon them, O Lord.
Be merciful unto them.
Hear us, O Lord.
From all suffering, *O Lord, deliver them.*
From all delay . . .
From the rigor of Thy justice . . .
From the gnawing pain of conscience . . .
From fearful darkness . . .
From their mourning and tears . . .
By Thy Incarnation . . .
By Thy Nativity . . .
By Thy own sweet Name . . .
By Thy Baptism and holy fasting . . .
By Thy most profound humility . . .

By Thy perfect submission . . .

By Thy infinite love . . .

By Thy anguish and torment . . .

By Thy bloody sweat . . .

By Thy bonds and chains . . .

By Thy crown of thorns . . .

By Thy ignominious Death . . .

By Thy sacred Wounds . . .

By Thy Cross and bitter Passion . . .

By Thy glorious Resurrection . . .

By Thy admirable Ascension . . .

By the coming of the Paraclete . . .

In the day of judgment, *We beseech Thee, hear us.*

Sinners as we are . . .

Thou who didst absolve the adulteress and pardon the good thief . . .

Thou who savest by Thy grace . . .

Thou who hath the keys of death and of hell . . .

That it may please Thee to deliver our parents, friends, and benefactors from torments . . .

That it may please Thee to deliver all the faithful departed . . .

That it may please Thee to have mercy on all those who have none in this world to remember or pray for them . . .

That it may please Thee to have mercy on all and to deliver them from their pains . . .

That it may please Thee to fulfill their
    desires . . .
That it may please Thee to admit them
    amongst Thine elect . . .
King of dreadful majesty . . .
Son of God . . .
Lamb of God who takes away the sins of
    the world, *Give them rest!*

Memento of the Dead

May this enlightened piety ever remain firmly
rooted in the hearts of all Christians.

And may the day never come when they will
cease to follow beyond the grave with tender solicitude the souls of those they loved in life. They
are God's friends, dear to His Sacred Heart, living
in His grace and in constant communion with Him.
Amen.

The Ringing of Bells

(The following excerpt explains the principal
functions of a bell as cited in the Prologue to
Longfellow's *Golden Legend*. Bells were rung to
give notice that a parishioner was in his or her
last agony and needed prayers. Bells were rung
again when a parishioner died in order that all
would pray in behalf of that individual's soul.

To this very day, in the village of Garabandal, Spain, the church bells are rung at seven in the evening to remind the people to pray for the holy souls in purgatory.)

I praise the true God,
I call the people,
I assemble the clergy,
I mourn the dead,
I disperse storm clouds,
I do honor to feasts,
I proclaim peace after bloodshed.

Roll Call for the Dead

(The holy souls are sacred presences in our lives. In gratitude we pray for one another and those who have gone before us. "We will console the souls, dear Jesus! Let our prayers be as incense in your sight.")

Let us pray for:
The next soul to enter heaven. *Lord, have mercy on our dead.*
The soul who is undergoing greatest sufferings . . .
The soul whose liberation would give God the greatest glory . . .
The soul most abandoned . . .
The soul who has been longest in purgatory . . .

The one who would have to stay there the
longest . . .
The last soul to enter purgatory . . .
The one who lived the longest on earth . . .
The one with the shortest earthly life . . .
The soul whom Jesus and Mary desire to
see freed most quickly . . .
The soul most devoted to Our Lord . . .
The soul most devoted to our Blessed
Mother . . .
The soul most devoted to St. Joseph . . .
The soul most devoted to all the saints . . .
The soul most devoted to St. Anne . . .
The one who prayed the most for sinners . . .
The one who prayed the most for the
lukewarm . . .
The one who prayed the most for the
sick . . .
The one who prayed the most for the
dying . . .
The one who prayed the most for the
deceased . . .
The one who prayed the most for our
separated brethren . . .
The one who prayed the most for
unbelievers . . .
The one who prayed the most for the
pope . . .
The one who prayed the most for the
missionaries . . .

The one who prayed the most for priests . . .
The one who prayed the most for his
parents and friends . . .
The one who prayed the most for
religious . . .
The one who prayed the most for rulers . . .
The one who prayed the most for officials
and soldiers . . .
The one who prayed the most for his
enemies . . .
The one who prayed the most for the poor
and the rich . . .
The soul for whom I am most obliged to
pray . . .
The souls who were my partners in sin . . .
Those to whom I was an occasion of sin . . .
The one who did me the most good
spiritually . . .
The one who did me the most good
materially . . .
The most outstanding in the love of
God . . .
The most outstanding in the love of
neighbor . . .
The most outstanding in humility . . .
The most outstanding in kindness . . .
The most outstanding in patience . . .
The most outstanding in resignation . . .
The most outstanding in temperance . . .
The most outstanding in compassion . . .

The most outstanding in faith . . .

The most outstanding in hope . . .

The one who sinned the most because of pride . . .

The one who sinned the most because of anger . . .

The one who sinned the most because of envy and jealousy . . .

The one who sinned the most because of revenge or bitter hatred . . .

The one who sinned the most because of vanity . . .

The one who sinned the most because of immodesty . . .

The one who sinned the most because of injurious words . . .

The one who sinned the most because of useless words . . .

The one who sinned the most because of oaths or curses . . .

The one who sinned the most because of laziness . . .

The soul most like me . . .

Canticle of Simeon

Lord, now you let your servant go in peace; your word has been fulfilled. My own eyes have seen the salvation which you have prepared in the sight of every people: a light to reveal you to the nations and the glory of your people Israel. Glory to the Father, and to the Son, and to the Holy Spirit, now and forever. Amen.

Novena Prayers
for Every Day

The Suffering of the Holy Souls

Their suffering never ceases.
They suffer day and night.
Without any repose.

Poor Souls' Novena for Every Day
(These powerful prayers are
over two hundred years old.)

IMMORTAL GLORY

O most loving God, Father of mercies, God of infinite goodness, behold me humbly prostrate before Thy throne; I pray and beseech Thee to have pity on the holy souls that are in the pains of purgatory. Cast on them a look of mercy, free them from their pains, and put them in possession of the inheritance of heaven. Remember that they are the work of Thy hands, redeemed by the most precious Blood of Thy divine Son, Jesus: deal with them according to Thy infinite mercy. Hear, O Lord, the prayer I make to Thee with all confidence, through the merits of the Passion and death of Thy most dear Son, Jesus, that they may be consoled, and may enjoy without delay that immortal glory which Thou hast prepared for Thy elect. O merciful Lord, have pity upon them, according to our trust in Thee. Amen.

Sunday ❖ O Lord God omnipotent, I beseech Thee by the precious Blood which Thy divine Son Jesus shed in the garden, deliver the souls in purgatory, and especially that soul which is the most forsaken of all, and bring it into Thy glory, where it may praise and bless Thee forever. Amen.

Our Father . . . Hail Mary . . . Eternal Rest . . .

Monday ❖ O Lord God omnipotent, I beseech Thee by the precious Blood which Thy divine Son Jesus shed in His cruel scourging, deliver the souls in purgatory, and among them all, especially that soul which is nearest to its entrance into Thy glory, that it may soon begin to praise Thee and bless Thee forever. Amen.

Our Father . . . Hail Mary . . . Eternal Rest . . .

Tuesday ❖ O Lord God omnipotent, I beseech Thee by the precious Blood of Thy divine Son Jesus that was shed in His bitter crowning with thorns, deliver the souls in purgatory, and among them all, particularly that soul which is in the greatest need of our prayers, in order that it may not long be delayed in praising Thee in Thy glory and blessing Thee forever. Amen.

Our Father . . . Hail Mary . . . Eternal Rest . . .

Wednesday ❖ O Lord God omnipotent, I beseech Thee by the precious Blood of Thy divine Son Jesus that was shed in the streets of Jerusalem while He carried on His sacred shoulders the heavy burden of the cross, deliver the souls in purgatory and especially that soul which is richest in merits in Thy sight, so that, having soon attained the high place in glory to which it is destined, it may praise Thee triumphantly and bless Thee forever. Amen.

Our Father . . . Hail Mary . . . Eternal Rest . . .

THURSDAY ❖ O Lord God omnipotent, I beseech Thee by the precious Body and Blood of Thy divine Son Jesus, which He Himself on the night before His passion gave as food and drink to His beloved Apostles and bequeathed to His holy Church to be the perpetual Sacrifice and life-giving nourishment of His faithful people, deliver the souls in purgatory, but most of all, that soul which was most devoted to this Mystery of infinite love, in order that it may praise Thee together with Thy divine Son and the Holy Spirit in Thy glory forever. Amen.

Our Father . . . Hail Mary . . . Eternal Rest . . .

FRIDAY ❖ O Lord God omnipotent, I beseech Thee by the precious Blood which Thy divine Son Jesus shed this day upon the tree of the cross, especially from His sacred hands and feet, deliver the souls in purgatory, and particularly that soul for whom I am most bound to pray, in order that I may not be the cause which hinders Thee from admitting it quickly into the possession of Thy glory where it may praise Thee and bless Thee forevermore. Amen.

Our Father . . . Hail Mary . . . Eternal Rest . . .

Saturday ❖ O Lord God omnipotent, I beseech Thee by the precious Blood which gushed forth from the sacred side of Thy divine Son Jesus in the presence and to the great sorrow of His most holy Mother, deliver the souls in purgatory, and among them all, especially that soul which has been most devoted to this noble Lady, that it may come quickly into Thy glory, there to praise Thee in her, and her in Thee through all the ages. Amen.

Our Father . . . Hail Mary . . . Eternal Rest . . .

Novena for the Holy Souls in Purgatory
(By St. Alphonsus de Liguori.)

Let us commend to Jesus Christ and His holy Mother the souls in purgatory, in particular those of our relatives, benefactors, friends, and enemies; especially for whom we are bound to pray; and let us offer the following considerations and prayers for them, pondering over the great sufferings which these spouses of Christ endure.

First Day ❖ Manifold are the sufferings which those blessed souls must endure, but the greatest of all is the reflection that their sins in life are the cause of their present torment.

Prayer: O Jesus, my Savior, I have so often deserved to be cast into hell; how great were my sufferings if I were now cast away and obliged to think that I, myself, had caused my damnation! I thank

Thee for the patience with which Thou hast endured me. My God, I love Thee above all things and I am heartily sorry for having offended Thee because Thou art infinite goodness. I would rather die than offend Thee again. Grant me the graces of perseverance; have pity on me and at the same time on those blessed souls suffering in purgatory.

O Mary, Mother of God, come to their assistance with thy powerful intercession.

Our Father . . . Hail Mary . . .
O most sweet Jesus, have mercy on them!
On Thy spouses have compassion,
on these suffering children Thine;
make these holy souls partakers
of Thy happiness Divine.

SECOND DAY ❖ The second pain which causes these holy souls much suffering, is the time lost in life, when they might have gained merits for Heaven, and the thought that they are unable to repair this loss, because the time of life and merit is passed.

Prayer: Woe to me, unhappy being, so many years have I already spent on earth and have earned naught but hell! I give Thee thanks, O Lord, for granting me time even now to atone for my sins. My good God, I am heartily sorry for having offended Thee. Send me Thy assistance, that I may apply the time yet remaining to me for Thy love and service; have compassion on me, and at the same time, on the holy souls suffering in purgatory.

O Mary, Mother of God, come to their assistance with thy powerful intercession.

Our Father . . . Hail Mary . . .
O most sweet Jesus, have mercy on them!
On Thy spouses have compassion,
on these suffering children Thine;
make these holy souls partakers
of Thy happiness Divine.

THIRD DAY ❖ Another great pain of the holy souls is caused by the hideous vision of their guilt, for which they now suffer. In this life the hideousness of sin is not seen as in the life to come; and this is one of the greatest sufferings of purgatory.

Prayer: O my God! Because Thou art infinite goodness, I love Thee above all things, and repent with my whole heart of my offenses against Thee. Grant me the grace of holy perseverance. Have compassion on me, and, at the same time, on the holy souls suffering in purgatory. O Mary, Mother of God, come to their assistance with thy powerful intercession.

Our Father . . . Hail Mary . . .
O most sweet Jesus, have mercy on them!
On Thy spouses have compassion,
on these suffering children Thine;
make these holy souls partakers
of Thy happiness Divine.

FOURTH DAY ❖ The pain that still more afflicts these holy souls, the spouses of Jesus, is the thought of having, during life, displeased by their sins that God whom they so ardently love.

Some penitents have felt so much pain and sorrow in thinking of having, by their sins, offended so good a God, that they died of grief. The souls in purgatory understand, far better than we do, the claims that God has to our love; they love Him with all their strength. Hence, at the thought of having offended Him during life, they experience pain that surpasses all other pain.

Prayer: O my God! Because Thou art infinite goodness, I am sorry with my whole heart for having offended Thee. I promise to die rather than ever offend Thee more. Give me holy perseverance; have pity on me, and have pity on those holy souls that anguish in the cleansing flames of love, and who love Thee with all their hearts.

O Mary, Mother of God, come to their assistance with thy powerful intercession.

Our Father . . . Hail Mary . . .
O most sweet Jesus, have mercy on them!
On Thy spouses have compassion,
on these suffering children Thine;
make these holy souls partakers
of Thy happiness Divine.

FIFTH DAY ❖ Another great suffering is caused these holy souls by the ignorance of the time of their deliverance. They are certain of being one day released, yet the uncertainty of the time when their purgatorial term will have ended gives them great pain.

Prayer: Woe to me, unhappy being, if Thou, O Lord, had cast me into hell; for from that dungeon of eternal pain there is no deliverance. I love Thee above all things, O infinite God, and I am sincerely sorry for having ever offended Thee again. Grant me the grace of holy perseverance. Have compassion on me, and, at the same time, on the holy souls in purgatory.

O Mary, Mother of God, come to their assistance with thy powerful intercession.

Our Father . . . Hail Mary . . .
O most sweet Jesus, have mercy on them!
On Thy spouses have compassion,
on these suffering children Thine;
make these holy souls partakers
of Thy happiness Divine.

Sixth Day ❖ The holy souls are, indeed, comforted by the recollection of the passion of Jesus Christ, and the Holy Sacrament of the Altar, since they know they are saved by the passion of Jesus Christ, and have received, and still receive, so much consolation from Holy Masses and Holy Communions. Nevertheless, they are greatly pained by the recollection of their ingratitude for these two gifts of love of Jesus Christ.

Prayer: O my Divine Redeemer, Thou didst die for me on the Cross, and have so often united Thyself with me in Holy Communion, and I have repaid Thee only with ingratitude. Now, however, I love Thee above all things, O supreme God; and I am more grieved at my offenses against Thee than any other evil. I would rather die than offend you again. Grant me the grace of holy perseverance. Have compassion on me and, at the same time, on the holy souls in purgatory.

O Mary, Mother of God, come to their assistance with thy powerful intercession.

Our Father . . . Hail Mary . . .
O most sweet Jesus, have mercy on them!
On Thy spouses have compassion,
on these suffering children Thine;
make these holy souls partakers
of Thy happiness Divine.

SEVENTH DAY ❖ A further great sorrow of these holy souls consists in their ardent desire for the beatific vision. Slowly and painfully the moments of their purgatorial imprisonment pass by, for they love God deeply and desire to be delivered from their sad prison in order to praise Him forever.

Prayer: O God, Father of Mercy, satisfy this their ardent desire! Send them Thy holy angel to announce to them, that Thou, their Father, art now reconciled with them through the suffering and death of Jesus, and that the moment of their deliverance has arrived.

O Mary, Mother of God, come to their assistance with thy powerful intercession.

Our Father . . . Hail Mary . . .
O most sweet Jesus, have mercy on them!

On Thy spouses have compassion,
on these suffering children Thine;
make these holy souls partakers
of Thy happiness Divine.

EIGHTH DAY ❖ Another bitter sorrow of these souls is caused by the reflection that God had distinguished them by so many graces not granted to others, and that they compelled Him, by their sins, to condemn them to these sufferings, and that they had deserved hell, and were pardoned and saved only by the mercy of God.

Prayer: O my God! I also am one of these ungrateful beings, having received so much grace, and yet despised Thy love, and deserved to be cast by Thee into hell. Thy infinite goodness has spared me until now. Therefore, I now love Thee above all things, and I am heartily sorry for having offended Thee. I would rather die than ever again offend Thee. Grant me the grace of holy perseverance. Have compassion on me and, at the same time, on the holy souls suffering in purgatory.

O Mary, Mother of God, come to their assistance with thy powerful intercession.

Our Father . . . Hail Mary . . .
O most sweet Jesus, have mercy on them!
On Thy spouses have compassion,
on these suffering children Thine;
make these holy souls partakers
of Thy happiness Divine.

NINTH DAY ❖ Great are all the sufferings of the holy souls: the fire, the grief, the darkness, the uncertainty of the time of their deliverance from prison; but the greatest of all these sorrows is this, that these holy souls are separated from their divine Spouse, and deprived of His beatific vision.

Prayer: O my God! How was it possible that I, for so many years, have borne tranquilly the separation from Thee and Thy holy grace! O infinite Good, how long-suffering hast Thou shown Thyself to me! Henceforth, I shall love Thee above all things. I am deeply sorry for having offended Thee. Grant me the grace of holy perseverance and do not allow that I should ever again fall into sin.

Have compassion on the holy souls in purgatory. I pray Thee, moderate their sufferings; shorten the time of their misery; call them soon unto Thee in heaven, that they may behold Thee face to face and forever love Thee.

O Mary, Mother of Mercy, come to their assistance with thy powerful intercession, and pray for us also who are still in danger of eternal damnation.

Our Father . . . Hail Mary . . .
O most sweet Jesus, have mercy on them!
On Thy spouses have compassion,
on these suffering children Thine;
make these holy souls partakers
of Thy happiness Divine.

About the Author

Susan Tassone holds a master's degree in religious education from Loyola University of Chicago. She is a consultant for a major nonprofit organization in the Windy City and has worked tirelessly to raise donations for Masses for the holy souls. Her first work, *The Way of the Cross for the Holy Souls in Purgatory*, was published by Our Sunday Visitor in 2000, of which more than 60,000 copies have been sold. Contact Our Sunday Visitor (toll-free: 1-800-348-2440, ext. 3; website: www.osv.com) and ask for these works by Susan Tassone:

- **The Way of the Cross for the Holy Souls in Purgatory,** 978-1-59276-141-8 (T192), hardback, 64 pages.
- **Praying in the Presence of Our Lord for the Holy Souls**, 978-0-87973-921-8 (921), paper, 176 pages.
- **The Rosary for the Holy Souls in Purgatory**, 978-1-931709-42-2 (T25), paper, 192 pages.
- **Thirty-Day Devotions for the Holy Souls**, 978-1-59276-052-7 (T103), paper, 160 pages.
- **Prayers for Eternal Life**, 978-1-59276-196-8 (T247), hardback, 64 pages.
- **Prayers of Intercession for the Holy Souls**, 978-1-59276-054-1 (M105), audio; 978-1-59276-055-8 (M106), CD.